DRAMAWISE
AN INTRODUCTION TO GCSE DRAMA

JOHN O'TOOLE AND BRAD HASEMAN

HEINEMANN
EDUCATIONAL

D1379476

Heinemann Educational Books Ltd
Halley Court, Jordan Hill, Oxford OX2 8EJ

OXFORD LONDON EDINBURGH
MADRID ATHENS BOLOGNA PARIS
MELBOURNE SYDNEY AUCKLAND SINGAPORE TOKYO
IBADAN NAIROBI HARARE GABORONE
PORTSMOUTH (NH) (USA)

First published 1987 in Heinemann Educational Australia
This edition first published 1988

94 95 13 12 11 10 9 8 7 6

ISBN 0 435 18036 3

Designed by Chris Haddon
Illustrated by Kevin Burgemeestre
Edited by Janet Blagg
Typeset by Times Graphics, Singapore
Printed in Great Britain by Thomson Litho Ltd, East Kilbride, Scotland.

Contents

Introduction

Gavin Bolton, Reader in Drama in Education, University of Durham

This must surely be the most useful book on drama to have come on the market. No other publication has managed, in the way this one does, both to stimulate dramatic action and to expose the dramatic principles behind that action. This is not a text merely offering a hundred ideas or tips for teachers which so many "practical handbooks" tend to do (leaving students high on action but low on understanding). And yet, paradoxically, it is essentially practical.

The format of the book is unique. Everything about it is double-edged. It is ostensibly aimed at students who want to take the initiative in conducting their own classroom drama and yet it will be a godsend to teachers; it seems to be about getting drama started, but the opportunity to sustain drama work of real quality and depth is also there; it is light-hearted in style inviting the students to "have fun" and yet is very serious in teaching the students that drama is the art of constraint; it seems to have an improvisational bias but suddenly we are working on scripts; we may think it's about a drama process but really it's about theatre. It is this latter paradox that is perhaps the key to the whole book for here, (at last!) we have a publication which demonstrates unequivocally the unity of drama and theatre and of process and product.

That unity pervades every section of the book for the authors, while introducing each chapter with attractive, easily manageable exercises, also cleverly illuminate the purposes of the exercises by reference to an excerpt from a play text, thus showing how a playwright (of both classical and contemporary genre) has followed the very same principles necessary to carrying out the most simple A and B pairs work. Improvisation and theatre merge into each other.

But it is the basis on which the sections are selected that gives intellectual rigour to the book. For the authors have modelled their sequence of chapters on a theory of drama which is set out in diagrammatic form at the beginning so that the reader can follow the rationale underpinning the choice of chapter headings. This is a brilliant conception for it means that the students are introduced to sound theoretical principles of drama/theatre irrespective of the level of their interest.

Those who subsequently take examinations in Drama will have been given a very good grounding. This is particularly relevant for GCSE students, for not only does the book provide insight into the nature of the subject, it provides the student with the appropriate language with which to discuss their own and other people's drama. They will absorb the language of dramatic criticism without realising it — the informality of the authors' unstuffy style belies the seriousness of their intent. Words such as tension, focus and symbolisation will not become artificial labels but vivid concepts rooted in experience.

Dramawise will give students an "academic training" in the very best sense of that phrase.

I believe it to be an astonishing achievement. If students, teachers, actors or academics really want to understand "the bones of drama" then this book is essential reading.

Notes for teachers

Drama is a creative, purposeful and disciplined art. If it is worth doing it is worth more than merely dabbling in. As the water gets deeper, so the person who has learned to swim is freer than the dabbler in the shallows.

This sequenced and structured book is actually about autonomy for the student. We want to give young people the tools of the trade so they can approach drama with the freedom and confidence of understanding — tools that artists (and teachers) often reserve themselves. You will not find 'skits' in this book, although you will find plenty of activity. The theoretical underpinning emerges through action that is significant, not trivial. Fun, certainly, but purposeful fun.

The key

Common to all dramas are certain elements and structures. These we have tried to identify, and set in an order where they can be explored simply and clearly through dramatic action.

The model of the elements of drama (opposite p. 1) is the key to the book. There is a chapter devoted to each element. After an understanding of each element has been developed through improvisation, we include a section, *And in Plays* ..., where extracts from well-known play texts, demonstrating the element in stage action, are offered as a further challenge to students.

The action

There is as little expository text as possible: we have chosen to work primarily through the dramatic process — through improvisation and exercise — so that the students can create and directly participate in lots of dramatic action. Isolated exercises are few; most of the improvisations build into significant dramas, step by step. We have not addressed style, genre, characterisation or production aspects specifically, nor are we primarily concerned with acting skills.

Whilst we have not explicitly addressed specific ideological issues either, we acknowledge that a very significant function of the art form of drama is the exploration of important and possibly contentious issues. However, particular issues are crucial for particular students and their teachers. The contexts of drama (and the contexts we have chosen) are in this sense arbitrary — the same elements are always present whatever the subject matter. As mastery of those elements develops, students will be empowered to raise their own issues through drama. In the final two chapters we deliver that process into the hands of the students.

Using this book

This book is developmental, and is designed to be implemented over about two years. We recommend that it be worked through sequentially — beginning with 'Preliminaries — the bones of drama'. The sequence of activities provides practical learning opportunities for students and teachers. It is essential that the teacher has a clear idea of the design and purpose of each activity before introducing it to the students.

Activities can be set up by the teacher or the students, although those activities which become major dramas will be strengthened if the teacher takes on a role and enters the action. An enthusiasm and willingness in the teacher to participate helps create a good atmosphere for drama.

The activities in this book have been used and developed with a large number of students in a wide range of teaching situations. We know from that experience that they work. However, if a set of activities or a drama fails to interest students, then the teacher may choose to devise a more suitable replacement.

Many teachers (and students) will have their own favourite activities and play texts which they may wish to use in preference to ours. The conceptual framework of this book will provide a helpful vehicle for this.

Documentation

Both documenting drama and transforming it into writing or other permanent media are valuable activities in themselves. They fix understanding of the drama, they help create reflective and critical habits, and they can feed back directly into the action. For this reason documentation is an essential part of a coherent drama course, and care needs to be taken to ensure that students are given adequate time, space, materials and privacy to realise its potential.

Most of the GCSE Drama Syllabuses involve documenting coursework as part of their assessment. One of the most common and useful ways of analysing dramatic action is to write reviews of plays seen. The analytical and critical skills needed for reviewing will be further developed when students undertake tasks which grow directly out of the action and document their thoughts and feelings.

Documentation has several distinct purposes:

1 In an improvised drama, it may form part of the dramatic action — writing a secret message, or devising a passport form for instance.

2 It may help a participant in an improvised drama, or an actor rehearsing a play, to increase belief. Making the context more specific — starting a drama of an epic voyage for instance by researching and charting the route and its dangers — may help to make the dramatic setting more real. Writing a letter to one's children before the forthcoming voyage could assist in deepening the enrolment by demanding a personal commitment.

3 Personal and reflective documentation of the drama helps the participants to clarify their attitudes and stances to the drama and the context. This may be in role — as a character in the drama writing to the newspapers, composing a song of triumph or writing an obituary.

4 Standing outside the action after it is over and evaluating the quality of what has gone on develops evaluation skills. Students record in a journal how the dramatic form was realised and make judgements about the effectiveness of the artistic decisions they made.

5 Further processing of the drama may take the form of turning it into a fixed performance, and developing a script, or of transforming it into another medium, such as a puppet play, story, artwork or exhibition.

6 As the contexts of drama go beyond the confines of the immediate time and place of each scene, many dramas need research, background data or material to back up an argument. Effective note taking, data gathering and recording often go hand in hand with effective drama, adding to the verisimilitude and deepening the dilemmas. (However, it is important to remember that a drama is in any case a *simplified* model of reality, and a clutter of data is not automatically an aid to truth.)

Whether working for GCSE coursework or not, in any coherent course of drama study, time should be made for the students to keep a regular diary or log of activities and responses. Here they can expose or give vent to their personal feelings on the drama, make judgements about the success and quality of their work, reflect on the workings of their group and the part they play in negotiation and decision-making.

In this book documenting tasks of many kinds are embedded within the activities, as naturally and interestingly as possible, with their purposes made plain.

— In Chapter 1 **documenting** is introduced, together with the concept that this may be done from *outside* the drama, or *within* it. A later activity introduces the distinction between *public* and *private* documentation.

— In Chapter 3 this is expanded to incorporate non-writing media like television and radio.

— Sustained reflective writing, in and out of role, is introduced within the central drama of Chapter 5.

— Chapter 7 introduces the notion of research beyond the drama to help create understanding and a point of view.

— Chapter 10 extends this notion into the drama itself, to show how a combination of dramatic exploration, research and creative documentation can all interlock with each other, and to investigate how drama can assist in developing understanding of the world beyond the students' experience, and a thoughtful personal ideology.

— The final two chapters both stress the importance of documentation throughout the drama course. Chapter 11 highlights the function of a student's journal in analysing structure, chronicling the progress and predicting future directions of a drama. In Chapter 12, the students are given an introduction to processing drama into a scripted play.

Assessment

Educational systems require drama teachers to judge the quality of student work. As we do so, care needs to be taken to use assessment techniques and criteria which are neither irksome nor destructive to our art. Exactly what to assess is of major importance.

Trying to make judgements on the individual's felt response and personal emotional growth always poses problems: we could find ourselves failing students because they are poor examples of themselves! All students need to participate with an integrity of affective response, and we need to base our judgements on the effective expression, appropriation, management and control of the medium demonstrated by the students.

There is a range of techniques which can be used to assess the different aspects of a student's work.

1 **Analysing role-play:** note signals and energy. Check for appropriateness, commitment and control.
2 **In-role documentation:** letters, diaries, photographs, newspaper articles, sketches, art work.
3 **Re-enactment:** replaying an incident accurately, for reporters, police.
4 **Transformation into performance:** communicating to an audience — live, video, audio.

5 Student journal: comments on the way the medium is being managed, future directions for the drama.

6 Out of role documentation: reflective writing, poetry, visual art work, newspaper report.

Criteria

It takes time and constant reappraisal to develop meaningful and reliable criteria for assessment. The sequencing of this book should help you and your students in this formative assessment. In addition, we have found the following criteria useful.

• Within the dramatic action, look for the ability in the student to:

1   understand the fiction
2   establish and sustain role
3   understand the implications of the human context and respond to the issues raised
4   maintain commitment to the central tension
5   respond constructively to changes in tension
6   initiate action to alter tension
7   work within the group focus
8   provide a focus for dramatic action
9   constructively modify space
10 respond to changes in established tempo
11 initiate changes in timing and tempo
12 perceive and respond to the mood appropriately
13 perceive and strengthen symbols in the drama
14 take care of the whole action of the drama.

• Outside the dramatic action, look for the ability to:

1   initiate ideas and organise future action
2   work with openness and assertiveness
3   critically evaluate dramatic action
4   work with commitment and purpose
5   manage criticism constructively.

The elements of drama

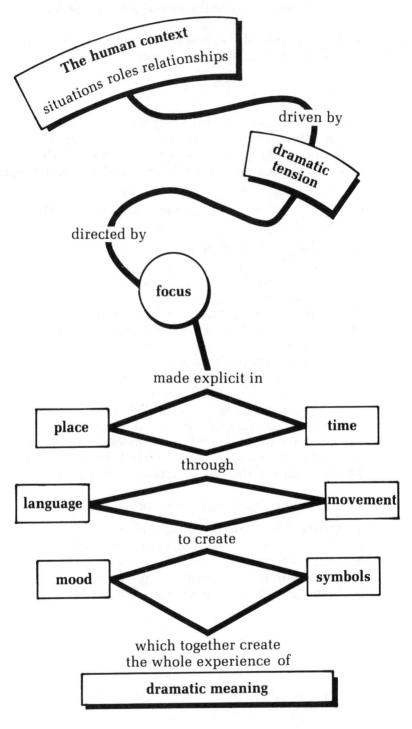

The human context
situations roles relationships

driven by

dramatic tension

directed by

focus

made explicit in

place — time

through

language — movement

to create

mood — symbols

which together create
the whole experience of

dramatic meaning

All dramas are fictional models of real life human behaviour

Preliminaries: the bones of drama

Wherever there are people, there is drama. Other people in other times have acted and danced their religion, their triumphs, their hates, their fears, their heroes. In our time too, we watch dramas enacted on the stage and screen and mimic our teachers, friends, bosses.

On television and in the theatre, drama has a *public face*, written and rehearsed before it is presented, But drama has a *private face* too:

- When we imitate our teachers or bosses we are relieving our feelings.
- When young children play mothers and fathers, or pirates and dragons, they are learning about power and responsibility, love and fear.
- When generals and armies play strategic exercises, they are asking: 'what would happen if . . .?' And nobody gets hurt.

And nobody watches.

Public or private, all drama has a purpose: and all drama has a structure — a skeleton. Your ideas and purposes will flesh out the bones; and through a series of active exercises and games, role-plays and improvisations, this book will help you make the skeleton dance.

You will see that you are asked simply to perform plays. There are opportunities to do so, of course, and your understanding of drama will be extended through performance, but the most exciting discoveries of drama are made when participants agree to step into an imagined world of their own making.

How this book works

Look at the skeleton diagram on the page opposite, showing the elements of drama. This is the key to this book. If you look at the chapter headings you can see that they match up with the key elements in the 'skeleton'. In the book, as in the diagram, each element emerges from the last and is the foundation for the next.

1

Each chapter explores and explains one of the elements of drama through practical activities using improvisation and role-play. After these activities, there is a section called 'And in plays ...' which shows how each element works in performance drama — that is, drama for an audience. This time the practical activities relate to well-known plays.

As you work through the activities you will find some of them grow into challenging and sustained dramas — complete in themselves. By the end of the book you will be creating your own dramas — for yourselves and for others.

How the drama group works

Drama works best when all members of a group trust each other and feel at ease together. Then everyone will be prepared to listen, to speak out, and to offer and accept criticism of ideas and work. Giving criticism without putting others down, and accepting criticism without becoming upset, are essential for effective group work. All members should be unafraid to express opinions, but at the same be sensitive to the others in the group.

Co-operation is the best way to share ideas and build the action. Your group may be required to work together out of class time. Everyone needs to attend these sessions. Group trust quickly breaks down when a member refuses to take part or is unreliable, arriving late and finishing early. When this happens, the group's energy is diverted from the drama work to handling this lack of commitment.

If you all make a strong commitment to your group and its tasks then you will find the drama highly enjoyable and rewarding. Your success depends upon how seriously you commit yourself to your group and the dramatic action you create.

1 The human context

Working in drama involves stepping into an imagined world. To make this imaginary world of drama meaningful and purposeful, it must have aspects of the real world in it. The central, real-world component of dramatic situations is human relationships.

Relationships and role

Relationships are central to all dramatic action:
- relationships between people
- the relationship between people and ideas
- the relationship between people and the environment.

We are able to set up relationships in our dramas by taking on roles. Role-playing does not demand elaborate acting skills — when you take on a role you are simply representing a point of view. You can portray this simply, honestly and as yourself, without elaborate costumes and props. You need not 'act' the part with special voices and funny walks.

Taking on a role involves identifying with a particular set of values and attitudes, which may or may not be your own. For example:

- the attitude of someone excited about the next royal visit
- the attitude of a parent who constantly argues with his or her adolescent daughter
- the attitude of someone who wants nuclear weapons banned.

Activity 1

1 Get into groups of three and decide who is **A**, **B** and **C**.

2 Each group member is to take one of the roles listed above, each choosing a different role.
- the royalist: 'Do you remember when the Queen came here?
- the despairing parent: 'I don't know why my daughter is so cheeky. We seem to fight all the time.'
- the nuclear disarmer: 'I don't want my child born deformed.'

3 Take them one at a time as follows:
- **A** takes on the chosen role. **A** starts with the sentence given above, and holds a conversation with **B** and **C** who should just be themselves (they can agree or disagree). Sustain the role-play for a whole minute, then cut it.
- Change now to **B** in his or her role, who will have a conversation with **A** and **C** as themselves.
- Change now to **C** in his or her role, who will have a conversation with **A** and **B** as themselves.

Accepting the fiction

How did those role-plays work? If you found yourself laughing or giggling, it probably means you were not trying hard enough to believe in the point of view of the role.

If drama is to work effectively for you and your group, accepting the fiction is essential. At first, this may seem difficult — you may feel silly accepting that your friend is your father, for instance, even in a drama. But this will soon pass, and as your experience with drama grows you will find yourself participating with ease. After all, we change roles constantly in real life. Think of how many roles you play in one day:

- how you act and speak in the Headteacher's office
- what you do and say in the tuck shop queue
- how you behave and talk with your grandparents.

All different; and all different faces of you. This adaptability in real life is a crucial aspect of drama.

Always respect the role you are playing — somebody, somewhere, really believes in the point of view you are presenting, and that person might be right. Thinking like this may help you to stay serious.

Features of role-playing

These next exercises will give you practice in taking on a role and developing relationships. As you work, watch out for the following:

1 You will need to think on your feet

You need to be responsive to the ideas of others and to the cues and signals they send to you about your role.

Activity 2

The role circle

1 All students stand in a circle.

2 Select one student to be in role as an investigating detective. The detective is going to question the students about a make-believe incident.

3 The detective enters the circle, introduces himself or herself, and explains that this investigation is into an incident which occurred last Friday night. Then the detective fires short, clear questions to students in the circle, so that a story is built.

4 You must respond to the detective's questions so that a sensible story emerges. You must take care to give only responses which tally with what people have already said. Listen to and remember the answers given to the detective's questions. Remember you are all establishing the one role.

For example:
Detective: (to a student) What's your name?
Student 1: Mary
Detective: (to a second student) Mary who?
Student 2: Johnson
Detective: (to a third student) Mary Johnson, where were you at 7 pm on Friday night?
Student 3: In town with my friends.
Detective: (to a fourth student) How many friends?
Student 4: Two others.

Cont.

Detective: (to a fifth student) Who saw the fire first?
Student 5: I did.
. . . and so on.

5 Run this investigation as quickly as possible, and cut after two or three minutes, when the role and the incident have been made clear.

6 Repeat this exercise with new detectives and new incidents.

2 You will need to negotiate your role

As you interact with others, you will have the opportunity to accept, reject or modify their attempts to shape your character. If, for example, it is said to you in role, 'Ah yes, you drive that green Ford,' you have a choice of responses. You could reply:

'Yes, I've had it two years.' (accepting the idea)
'No, I haven't even got my licence.' (rejecting the idea)
'Well I have been driving a green Ford, but it's my parents' car.' (modifying the idea).

This negotiation of the situation and roles is an important and necessary step in all drama.

Activity
3

1 Form into pairs. Decide who is **A**, who is **B**.

2 **A** moves away from **B** and stands somewhere else in the room.

3 **A**'s task is to think of a situation, then approach **B** and start a role-play. **A** will need a few seconds to think of the first line. Straightaway **A** must make clear:
  • the identities of both **A** and **B**
  • where they are
  • what they are there for.

4 Commence the exercise. Stop the role-play after two or three minutes (no longer!), and discuss how effective those first moments were. **B**: did you get clear signals from **A**?

5 Repeat the exercise with **B** offering a new situation. Cut after two minutes. Were the signals clear this time?

6 Separate again. This time **B** will adopt and hold a particular physical position (eg staring out of the window). Repeat the exercise, but now **A** must take into account **B**'s posture (eg 'Julia, watch out for the doctor. Call me the moment he arrives.') Cut after two minutes and discuss your roles.

7 Repeat with **A** holding the posture and **B** offering the situation.

Developing role

Stepping into role is a little like an actor working to create a character in a play or film. However, actors develop more than just a set of attitudes — they need to build a complex personality and background for their character, using a process called characterisation. In improvised drama, our needs are not as detailed. As we adopt the appropriate attitudes we say we have taken on the role of the character.

There are three basic aspects of role to take into account when improvising. These are purpose, status and attitude.

The purpose of the role

As you develop your role, it is helpful to keep in mind the *purpose* you have in the drama. A character's purpose may change, sometimes quite quickly. For example a character may start by seeking help or information from a relative, and end up giving support to that relative, who has just had a car accident.

Activity 4

Roles:	**A**: a young person your own age **B**: a middle-aged friend of the family
Context:	**A** is calling on **B**, to ask advice about a personal problem. **B** is very shaken after just hearing some bad news.
Management:	**1 A**: decide what your problem is — perhaps about money, a girlfriend or boyfriend, school-work, etc. **2 B**: decide what news you have just heard — perhaps a phone call from your daughter, or some news on television. These should both be sensible ideas that are likely to happen. Avoid being melodramatic. **3** **A** starts the role-play by approaching **B**, as if calling at the house. **4** Remember: you both have a purpose — you need to talk to each other — but your purpose may change. Remember also that you like and respect each other.
Outcome:	After three minutes stop the role-play: **B** has to answer the telephone. Briefly discuss with your partner whether you each achieved your purpose, or had to modify it.

The status of the role

All relationships have an element of power in them — this means that one person has some hold over the other, some special knowledge or a higher position. We call this status. You have to consider your roles, in relation to each other, in terms of status: will your role be of higher, lower or equal status?

- *Higher status*: are you the monarch, a bank manager, a computer expert, the gold medal winner returning from the Olympics?
- *Lower status*: are you about to receive a knighthood, needing a loan, needing your computer fixed, the athlete sent home early from the Olympics in disgrace?
- *Equal status*: are you all being knighted together, all bank managers together, all members of the Olympic team?

Your status will affect your manner and bearing towards the others in the drama.

Activity 5

Roles:	**A**: Branch Manager of the Amicable Bank **B**: a 17-year-old in his or her first job **C**: District Manager of the Amicable Bank
First context:	An interview between **A** and **B** in the Branch Manager's office. **B** wishes to borrow money from the bank, but the outcome depends on the interview.
Management:	**1** **B**: decide why you want the money and how much you want. Where do you work? How much are you earning in your job? (Be realistic!)
	2 **A**: you are prepared to make loans to young people, but you must be convinced that they are responsible citizens who have the ability to meet the repayments.
	3 **C**: just watch this scene, and see how the manager maintains the higher status, and the young person the lower.
Outcomes:	**1** Eventually, the manager will lend the money. **2** Manager **A**: write a brief report to attach to that customer's file, explaining what your doubts were, and why you finally decide to lend the money Young customer **B**: write to a friend triumphantly that you got the loan and include a brief account of how hard your interview was (and perhaps how much the manager used his higher status over you). Monitor **C**: just write an account of what

Cont.

you saw, picking out as accurately as you can examples of high and low status.

Second context: Some months later in the same manager's office. **A** is being reprimanded by **C**, the District Manager. Young **B** has proved to be a bad risk, and defaulted on repayments.

Management: **1** **C** wants to know why **A** lent the money to **B**, and accuses **A** of being a bad judge of character.
2 **B**: just watch the scene, and see how **A**'s behaviour changes when in the lower status position.

Outcomes: **1** Eventually **A** is forgiven, but not before being quite humiliated — and having to swallow it.

2 Briefly, out of role, share what you noticed about the difference in behaviour between the low and the high status characters. Look especially at the signals given out by **A**, who was still the same person in the same job, but with the status completely changed.

Documenting your work

Sometimes, in order to understand what is going on in our drama, tasks other than drama itself, like writing, may be helpful. In the dramas which follow, you will be writing, and also designing, building, making tapes and videos, etc., which will last beyond the life of the drama itself and become the relics or documents of the drama.

You will notice in this drama that you were asked to write after the first scene. We hope this helped you to fix the significance of the scene in your own minds. Some of the writing was even an important part of the drama itself. **A**'s report became part of the evidence which **C** used against **A**.

Each of the three characters writes something quite different, looking at the drama from their own point of view. You may notice, for instance, that **A** and **B** are both writing from *inside* the drama — still in role. **C**, obviously, is documenting the dramatic action from *outside*. This distinction is quite an important one, which we shall return to later.

The attitude of the role

Each character in every drama has attitudes towards, amongst other things, the subject of the drama and the other characters in the drama.

Regarding the subject matter of the drama, as prisoners-of-war, for example, some may hate the camp: it is a prison; while others may be content in the camp, safe from the dangers of combat.

In terms of the other characters of the drama, in the same prison camp some prisoners may hate the guards, while others may have a friendly attitude towards them, especially if they share a common background, or a common interest like sport. Of course it is important to have good reasons why you like or dislike the other characters in the drama.

Activity 6

Setting:	A prison camp — you decide which war.
Roles:	Four or five prisoners and two guards.
Context:	The guards have been ordered to organise all the prisoners into a concert party. The prisoners have already heard rumours about this.
Attitudes:	**1** The prisoners have a range of attitudes towards the concert: one may think it will relieve the boredom, another may think it is an attempt to humiliate them, a third may see a way of using it to help them escape, a fourth may just enjoy performing, etc.
	2 The guards have different attitudes too: one, who is friendly with many prisoners, is in favour of it; while the other, who hates the prisoners, and thinks the camp is not harsh enough, disapproves of it.
Management:	**1** Get into groups of six or seven and split into prisoners and guards. Find an appropriate space to represent the prison hut.
	2 Decide on what attitude you will take (it should be one you feel comfortable with and can believe). Make sure that everybody in the group knows which guard is friendly, which is harsh.

Cont.

3 In the hut the prisoners have a meeting to discuss the concert party plan. Outside, the guards discuss it too.

4 The guards enter, to tell the prisoners about the plan and to start organising them.

5 Remember, the guards have all the power, so avoid melodramatic conflicts.

Outcome: **1** Let this run until all the attitudes have become clear, then find a natural way to close it.

2 *Prisoners:*
- If you are in favour of the concert, write an article or advertisement for the camp newspaper, outlining the idea of the concert, and asking for volunteers to perform.
- If you do not support the concert, write a secret letter to your fellow prisoners, calling on them to boycott it.

Guards:
- If you are in favour, write your next letter home, telling your family about this pleasant diversion.
- If you do not support it, write that evening's entry in your personal diary.

Documenting for understanding

Again, there was a writing activity in this drama. Its purpose was to help you fix and express your final attitudes clearly. Often, writing them down is the best way for this.

Note, too, that the Guards and the Prisoners engaged in very different types of writing. While the Guards wrote personal and **private** statements, either for themselves or their close family, the Prisoners were expressing their attitudes to a more **public** audience (public, even though one group had to be at the same time secret!).

Drama creates many opportunities to write for both public and private audiences. As you will recall from the Banking scenes (Activity 5), we can also choose to write from inside, still in the role, or outside the dramatic action. In the prisoner-of-war camp drama, all the writing was from *inside* the action. Suppose we had asked you to, say, list the arguments for and against the concert, or to write about how you felt in the drama. These writing tasks would then have been from outside the action, the first for public sharing, the second a private record.

Motivation

Purpose, status and attitude all form part of the character's motivation. This refers to what the character hopes to achieve. Very often, in order to create a strong drama this goal is kept from the others in the drama. As a result we find characters may say and do one thing, while in fact they really believe and want something else. For example:

What seems to be going on	What is really going on
The council official expresses sympathy for the young couple who are afraid that the bypass will pass through their property.	The official, who designed the bypass, believes it to be in the best interests of the whole community, and cares little for the problems of the couple.
An older, married couple are urging a young woman to make up her mind and marry her boyfriend.	The couple are very unhappy in their marriage and trying not to let it show.

Sub-text

As you can see from these examples, all is not what it seems. We refer to what is said as the text of the role-play. The real intention, which lies unsaid beneath the text, is called the sub-text.

These concepts of text and sub-text are important for creating rich dramatic action. As you work through the activities in this book you will see how sub-text injects interest and an additional dimension to the drama.

And in plays . . .

Extract 1: from *The Fourth Year Are Animals* by Richard Tulloch

The first piece of text we will use, and several others in this book, come from Richard Tulloch's play *The Fourth Year Are Animals*. The very title helps to set the scene, and gives the audience some idea of what to expect. You might guess that it is set in a secondary school, features some fourth year students, and includes the point of view of some teachers. You would be right! It starts with Alan Howman's first day as a newly qualified teacher, meeting Kelly, one of his fourth formers.

> (*Outside the office* — ALAN *encounters* KELLY *in the playground.*)

ALAN: Excuse me — can you tell me where the office is?

KELLY: You a new teacher?

ALAN: That's right.

KELLY: What are you teaching?

ALAN: English I think.

KELLY: Hasn't Mrs Harrison told ya?

ALAN: Is that the Head?

KELLY: You want to see her?

ALAN: Yes, that's why I asked . . .

KELLY: You go down the end of this corridor, then there's these double doors that's the gym and then you turn down to your left and that's her office.

ALAN: Thanks.

> (*He starts to go.*)

KELLY: What's your name?

ALAN: Alan . . . Mr Howman. What's yours?

KELLY: You been at a school yet?

ALAN: Pardon?

KELLY: You been at a school yet?

ALAN: Have I been teaching at a school you mean?

KELLY: Yeah.

ALAN: Well yes — I've done some teaching practice while I was at College.

KELLY: This is your first job as a teacher though.

ALAN: Paid job, yes.

KELLY: Oh — hope we get you.

ALAN: You never know your luck.

(*KELLY exits.*)

As you prepare to perform

This scene can be performed in pairs, so that everybody has the chance to try it out. If you prefer, you can select two people to play Alan and Kelly, with the rest of the class helping them to set the scene up, and observing how it emerges.

Think about

Before you decide how Alan will 'encounter' Kelly, you will need to answer some questions about who they are, and, even though they are only just meeting for the first time, what their relationship is. Even as you read the dialogue with each other, you will be able to start answering these questions. Some of them are connected, and answering one will help you to answer others.

Relationships

1 Do they both seem friendly, or is one of them more friendly than the other? Why do you think this might be, if they have never met before?
2 Who is the more familiar and more confident with the situation? Why?

Status

1 Who is the senior?
2 Is one of them trying to gain power over the other? Why might this be? (You might notice that Kelly never answers Alan directly, and never tells him her name.)

Attitude

Look at them one at a time.
1   What is Alan's attitude to this student? Does it change during the scene?
2   What is Kelly's attitude to Alan? Does it change?

Motivation

1   Alan's main motivation is to find the way to the Head's office. However, Kelly is the first student he has met in the school, so what other purpose might he have in the way he speaks to her?
2   Is Kelly's main motivation just to give Alan the information he wants? What else might she be wanting to do?
3   Look at the line 'Oh — hope we get you.' Is Kelly just being polite, or has she got a sub-text? If so, what is it?
4   Have any of Alan's lines got a sub-text, do you think?

Try out the scene

Make a space that will represent the playground. It should be possible for the characters to start some distance apart.
   You should now have enough information about the characters, their roles and relationships to bring the scene to life. Start by deciding how Alan encounters Kelly — does he go over to her or does she bump into him? Now go on from there.

2 Dramatic tension

Like the rubber band which drives a model aeroplane, tension is the force which drives our drama. In some ways it is the hardest element of drama to grasp, because you cannot see it or touch it, you can only feel it; yet it is the most important element, and no drama exists without it — it must be created, and it can easily be lost.

Activity 1

1 Choose two volunteers: **A**'s task is to menace, then stab, **B** (in drama, not reality!).

2 With everybody else around the edge of the room, **A** and **B** stand in the middle, quite close together. **A**, perhaps angry, wants to do the stabbing as fast as possible. **B** initially backs away, then submits. Try it quickly.

You will find that it was exciting, but not very tense.

3 Choose another two volunteers. With **A** and everyone else at one end of the room and **B** at the other, try it again. This time **A** is more sadistic, moving very slowly and quite silently, holding the knife daintily.

You will probably notice that this time there was much more tension, and that the tension was in the approach, not the act.

Cont.

4 Now group everybody in a menacing horseshoe around **B**, and do it again, equally slowly, with the only sound that of everyone's fingers clicking in unison.
More tension still?

5 Can you find a way of prolonging the tension in the stabbing — perhaps by **B** pleading, or **A** improvising a motive for the act as the knife is slowly inserted, all the while holding eye contact, etc?

Creating tension

The scene you just created was very violent, but dramatic tension need not have anything to do with violence, nor even conflict — although there is often conflict in drama. There are four major means of creating and intensifying dramatic tension.

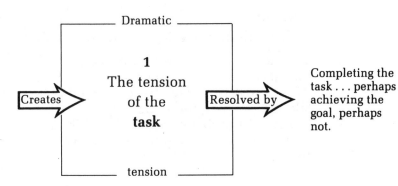

Dramatic tension

The problem of the task which the characters must complete. —Creates→ **1** The tension of the **task** —Resolved by→ Completing the task . . . perhaps achieving the goal, perhaps not.

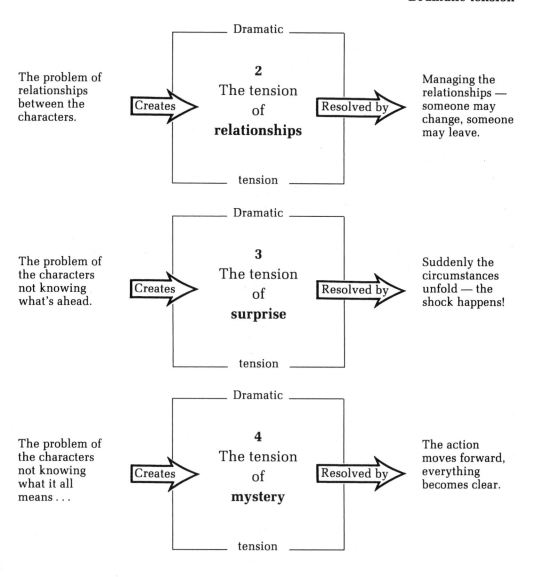

The problem of relationships between the characters. Creates → **2 The tension of relationships** Resolved by → Managing the relationships — someone may change, someone may leave.

The problem of the characters not knowing what's ahead. Creates → **3 The tension of surprise** Resolved by → Suddenly the circumstances unfold — the shock happens!

The problem of the characters not knowing what it all means... Creates → **4 The tension of mystery** Resolved by → The action moves forward, everything becomes clear.

There is also another, quite different, means of creating tension — but more of that later.

As we discuss each of the means of creating tension listed above, our practical activities will all be games. Games are similar to drama; they create tension (that's why they are so popular), so we will use them to enable you to feel the tension.

Tension of the task

Before the problem which is at the root of any dramatic situation can be resolved, the characters must do and say many things — perhaps change, for better or worse. Those are their tasks, and together they make up the action of the drama. To make the dramatic action tense, we must:

1 Make the task hard: if it's not, the play will be over straight away, and no-one will care about the outcome anyway.

Game 1

Artists everywhere!

1 Two students, **A** and **B**, are to work together.

2 **B** is to think of an object — a pencil case, a coffee cup, etc which **A** is to sketch. **A** does not know what the object is and will be blindfolded. **B** gives **A** instructions about how to draw the object, but cannot help beyond that.

3 **A**: try your hardest. As you draw, can you guess what the object is? Finally, take off the blindfold and compare the sketch with the real thing.

From game to drama: a dramatic situation creating a similar tension would be a deaf and dumb child who has witnessed a crime and has to be coaxed to draw what he or she saw. Can you devise a dramatic situation which would create a similar kind of tension? What situation could possibly include a person struggling to make sense of strange information?

2 Make the task important: resolving the problem must matter to those in the drama. There must be reasons why the problem is important. For example:
- this is urgent because . . .
- we must be secret in case . . .
- I have to do this otherwise we'll never know what . . .

3 Make the task fun: the best drama is always fun —serious fun. Don't forget to enjoy it.

Game 2

Winking for freedom

1 One student is selected to stand in the middle of the space. This person has great responsibility — he or she is the rescuer!

2   A circle of chairs is set out facing the rescuer, so that half the class can sit down. These students are the prisoners. The other students, standing behind the chairs, are the gaolers, who must prevent their prisoners from escaping.

3   The rescuer must now attempt to save the prisoners by winking at them. When a prisoner receives a wink, he or she must dive for the rescuer, out of the gaoler's clutches. If prisoners are tagged by their gaolers as they move they must return to their seat.

Can the rescuer free all the prisoners? Try: it's possible.

From game to drama: by naming the roles as 'rescuer', 'gaoler' etc, we have already started to give the game one possible dramatic context. What drama could you devise which builds on these feelings? Where could an attempted escape occur? Who is escaping? Why?

Tension of relationships

We have already seen that human relationships are the central component of the dramatic situation. So it follows that one of the most common sources of tension is to be found in the relationships which exist between characters. Tension can arise out of misunderstandings, dilemmas or conflict between people. It can also be found in the rituals that people share.

Misunderstanding

Misunderstandings, and the consequences which flow from them, provide the source of much dramatic tension. Misunderstandings can be accidental, where there is a genuine misunderstanding between characters, or deliberate, where one character deliberately hides something from another. The resolution of the misunderstanding and its resulting confusion, can work in two ways. In comedy, the consequences are inevitably funny; in tragedy, the consequences are disastrous.

Game
3

Who am I?

1   One student is selected to leave the room. While out of earshot, the rest of the group decide upon a character they

Cont.

wish the outsider to be. (Perhaps Florence Nightingale, perhaps John Lennon.)

2 The outsider returns and asks questions of each group member in an effort to discover the identity he or she has been given.

3 Members of the group can only answer 'Yes' or 'No' to the outsider's questions. They must also treat the outsider as if he or she really is the character.

4 The outsider finally declares his or her identity.

From game to drama: what dramatic situation could build on the outsider's feelings of uncertainty and confusion? Where could such a drama be located? How can people forget who they are? Why might they?

Intimacy

When someone confides in you, you often feel a degree of tension when you hear their secret. This is because a secret bonds people together — it is an act of trust. And the greater the secret, the greater the bond. The revealing of a secret, especially a grave one, is a moment of great tension.

Game
4

Find the hands

1 Form pairs of **A** and **B**.

2 Sitting opposite each other, **A** is to take **B**'s hands and explore them through touch, to get to know them by the way they feel. It will help if **A**'s eyes are closed while doing this.

3 **B** now takes **A**'s hands and explores them in the same way.

4 When **A** and **B** know their partner's hands well, form groups of six — three pairs. With all six blindfolded, explore all of the hands to find your partner. Be silent during this time. When you are sure you have your partner, take your blindfolds off.

Don't be surprised if you feel a strong urge to laugh during this exercise. This is quite normal — exploring someone else's hands in such a way is an intimacy not normally shared by people. In fact, the laughter is your discomfort trying to relieve the tension. It is essential that you don't laugh though — otherwise the tension will be lost completely.

From game to drama: what situation can you think of which involves two people, one holding the other's hands, sharing a private moment? What could the problem be?

Ceremony

A ceremony, or a ritual, carries its own tension, to do with:
- confirming the importance of the task
- the rightness and rhythms of doing the task in such a way
- the crucial fact that the ceremony is shared by all.

Many dramatic actions have something of ceremony about them — even the group stabbing of **B** in Activity 1 had a ritual quality.

Ceremony does not have to be grand. Many everyday actions in life have a ceremonial element — eating together, meeting people, going through Customs, bidding at an auction. It is important to create shared ritual moments in drama, which, of course, also help to slow down the dramatic action.

Game
5

The Court of the Holy Dido

This game uses an extremely formal situation to create tension.

1 One student is appointed the President of the Court of the Holy Dido. The President holds the Holy Dido (any object — but normally a rolled up newspaper). All stand in a circle, facing inwards.

Cont.

2 The President calls the members of the Court to order by announcing, 'Knights of the Court of the Holy Dido, this Court is now in session. Bow as the Holy Dido passes.'

3 The President then solemnly, and with great respect, parades the Holy Dido by walking around the circle; finally placing the Holy Dido in the centre of the circle and returning to his or her place.

4 From this time on all Knights of the Court must sit with their arms and legs crossed and not make a sound. They cannot do anything — smile, scratch or cough — without the permission of the President.

5 If a Knight breaks one of these rules, then punishment is dealt out by the President. The procedure for this is as follows:

- One Knight asks the President for permission to speak. If granted, that Knight lodges the complaint about the rule-breaker's behaviour by saying:
  'President of the Court, may I take the Holy Dido and punish Knight [Julie] for [smiling/coughing/licking her lips, etc] without the permission of the court.'
- The President then offers a ruling on this request, and gives sentence by saying:
  'Honourable Knight, I too saw the unworthy Knight [Julie] [smile/cough/lick her lips], and decree that she shall be struck twice, one blow on each hand. Take up the Holy Dido.'

6 After the punishment has been given, the Knight giving it must ask permission to return the Holy Dido. This must be done with the greatest care and respect.

7 The game continues in this way. The President can also direct one Knight to punish another if the Knights are slow in requesting punishment.

8 The game concludes when the President declares, 'This session of The Court of the Holy Dido is now closed.'

From game to drama: this quite complex game uses ceremony to create tension. What ceremonies are there in real life which create tension, for both the participants and observers? How could you use a ceremony in a dramatic situation to deepen dramatic tension?

Dilemma

The tension of dilemma results from the conflict within the situation. As characters strive to achieve their goals, they are often confronted by conflicting choices, called dilemmas, where decisions have to be made and consequences faced. The dilemma may be:
- moral — is it right to let this character escape?
- social — if we rescue Smith will it help or hinder us?
- personal — I am a gaoler, but I believe this person is innocent.

Solving one dilemma may lead on to another, maybe an even bigger one. The more awkward the situation, the harder the decision, and the more consequences have to be faced. Facing the consequences increases dramatic tension.

Game 6

Trust me — step this way!

1   The class is to break into three groups: **A**, **B** and **C**.

2   All members of group **A** are to be blindfolded. Groups **B** and **C** are to devise an obstacle course in the space, leaving an open path for **A** to follow.

3   Groups **B** and **C** should mix up and line the path. They must now call instructions to the members of group **A** as they enter the maze. Those in group **B** must help group **A** make its way through the maze, by calling accurate instructions. Group **C** must try to confuse group **A** by calling wrong instructions which will lead them into disaster.

4   Each member of group **A** must listen for a voice to trust in order to find a way out of the maze.

From game to drama: devise a drama which places some participants in a situation where they have to choose one course of action from a range of desirable (or undesirable!) alternatives. Advice can be given and received, but finally that hard decision must be made.

Conflict

Conflict is the easiest and most common way of creating tension, of preventing characters from achieving their goals. Conflict may be set up by making the goals opposing:

- a slave wants his freedom; his mistress wants unpaid workers
- a rock star wants to quit; her manager needs her income
- a woman wants a career; her husband wants babies.

Or the conflict may be one of attitudes within the same person:
- the slave hates his mistress but loves her children
- the rock star hates her manager, but knows he's the best in the business
- the woman wants a career and babies.

But, because it is the easiest source of tension, beware — conflict can lead you astray. Often personal conflicts and arguments can run away with the drama. They can become an end in themselves, because neither party is going to give in (and because it's just a drama, nobody can make you . . .). The goals disappear in shouting or violent confrontations, and a lot of slammed doors.

Conflict should be used sparingly, to enrich the other tensions, for example the tension of the task:
- how can the slaves revolt if their two leaders do not trust each other?

And the tension of dilemma:
- the slave hates slavery but loves the children of the mistress; he believes in the revolution, but does not want them to be killed.

Game 7

Knee boxing

1 Make pairs. Face each other, and with open hands attempt to slap the knees of your opponent. Treat this as a contest — who will be the winner?

2 Set up the contest again, this time in threes. Two can now work as a team to attack the third.

From game to drama: devise a drama around two people in direct conflict. What would be the effect of suddenly giving more power to one of the combatants? How could you do this in your drama?

Tension of surprise

One of the most common ways of injecting dramatic tension into action is suddenly to introduce a shock or surprise. The shock releases energy and excitement and the action quickly becomes richer. Surprise is often the result of something quite unexpected happening suddenly. But it can also arise when something that has been expected all along finally does come about.

Shock of the expected

You all anticipate that the inevitable will happen and desperately try to prevent it. You work hard and hatch plans, but when you think all will be OK — the expected happens! When the eviction letter arrives or the death warrant is signed you are confronted with what it means to you right now. Immediately, you and others are affected by it, reacting freshly to it.

Another aspect of this tension is that it builds while we wait. Waiting often adds to the tension, as we wonder if the expected will happen.

Grandmother's footsteps

This game requires a fairly large space.

1 One student, **A**, is selected to stand facing the wall at the far end of the space.

2 Starting from the other end of the room the other students are to advance, their task being to close on **A** and tap him or her on the shoulder, without being seen to move.

3 The group must advance cautiously, taking small steps only, as **A** can turn around at any time to spot people moving. Anyone so caught must return to the starting point.

From game to drama: in what dramatic situation could stalking the inevitable victim be planned, anticipated, and yet still cause surprise?

Shock of the unexpected

As the action unfolds and the characters pursue their tasks, something quite unpredictable happens:
- a stranger arrives bearing astonishing news
- some matter dealt with earlier rears its head again
- one of the characters reveals a new side.

This unexpected shock creates further tension. The most dramatic of these unexpected shocks comes when your expectations are reversed, when suddenly you are betrayed in some way or another. Suddenly you find:
- your escape plans blow up in your face as the tunnel leads . . . to the Asylum Wing
- the poor refugee you have sheltered turns out to be . . . a war criminal
- the wasteland you have reclaimed for the community is now going to be used for . . . a supermarket.

This kind of reversal can only be used late in the drama, after strong expectations have been established. And remember too that there is a limit to our capacity to be surprised. Moreover, without good care and a good reason, the surprise may be an anticlimax — a dud. So use it sparingly. In most dramas, tension is generated without the sudden energy of a shock. In these instances a build up of tension usually involves slowing down the action, rather than injecting a sudden crisis.

Game 9

Consequences

Each student needs a long sheet of paper and a pen.

1 With the group sitting in a circle, each person is to supply and write down certain information. After each piece of new information is added, the paper is folded so that the previous information is hidden. It is then passed to the student on the left. The next piece of information is added by that student. The pieces of information all add up to a story, to be read aloud at the end of the game.

2 Students must write nine pieces of information, which are:
- the name of a girl or woman (fold and pass)
- the word 'met' and the name of a boy or man (fold and pass)
- the word 'at' and the place they met (fold and pass)
- the words 'and she was' and an explanation of what she was doing (fold and pass)
- the words 'and he was' and an explanation of what he was doing (fold and pass)
- the words 'she said to him' and whatever she said (fold and pass)
- the words 'he replied' and whatever he said (fold and pass)
- the words 'and then they' and what they did (fold and pass)
- the words 'and the consequence was' and the details of the consequence (fold and pass).

From game to drama: the comic tension in this game comes from the unexpected twists in the story. Select any dramatic context you have created as part of the 'From games to drama' activities in this chapter, and plan a surprise, a shock, which you could inject to increase the dramatic tension.

Tension of mystery

Dramatic tension can be heightened by mystery; there is something we must discover (What does this mean? Where will this take us?), and secrecy; preventing others from finding out (What are they hiding from us? Is this the whole story?). Of course, we can still experience strong dramatic tension, even if we do know the outcome of the drama.

After all, most people who watch *Hamlet* or *Star Wars* have seen them before and know how they end (one hero dies, the other doesn't). However, it can be useful to build tension round those things which are left unknown, or are unknown to us now:

- What does this mean?
- What will happen next (beyond our control)?
- What will our action lead to?
- Why have they done this?

The unknown

There is an important distinction to be made between the role-player and the real character within a drama. For example, the players in a hostage drama may have decided beforehand that eventually the hostages will be released, but as terrorists and hostages none of them know that as they sit in the plane.

So you may find it helpful to distinguish between:

- what knowledge you as players have as you structure the drama
- what knowledge the characters would have
- the outcomes you leave the drama to decide, eg will the hostages escape?

Game 10

Wink murder

1 One student is selected to play the detective and leaves the room.

2 All other students sit in a circle and close their eyes. The teacher walks behind the circle and silently taps one student on the shoulder. This student will be the murderer.

3 With the detective in the centre of the circle, the game begins. The murderer first selects a victim by making eye contact and then winks at him or her. If you are winked at you're dead, and must die by falling to the floor.

4 The aim of the detective is to identify the murderer before too many bodies pile up. The murderer's task is to kill as many people as possible. The victims can try to spot the murderer — and enjoy dying if your wink comes up!

From game to drama: with a detective and murders, this game is well on the way to becoming a drama. Think of a way to use mystery and secrecy in a dramatic situation. In your situation, who knows something the others don't? How can suspicions be raised? What can the others do to find out?

Tension 5?

As we hinted earlier, there is, especially in improvised drama, a fifth tension, the tension between the world of the drama and the real world. Within a drama you may be freed to do what in real life you could not do, and this can add power to your participation in the drama:
- your character may need to use language normally taboo in the classroom
- your teacher may be playing the role of a helpless, ludicrous beggar
- a row, or a tender scene, may be fuelled by the real feelings of the players.

In an improvised drama in a South African school, a class of black students, in role as police and social workers, manhandled, stroked, cradled and carried a group of white teachers who were in role as drug addicts. The session held such tension and excitement that both groups found it hard to bear. In South Africa, white and black people hardly ever touch each other in real life. Come to that, how often have you experienced, even in Britain, physical contact between teachers and students?

And in plays . . .

Extract 3: from *The Children's Crusade* by Paul Thompson

The Children's Crusade tells of the attempted expedition to Constantinople made by thousands of children in the Middle Ages. In 1212 the child crusaders left Europe for the Holy Land, with the dream of freeing it from Muslim control. The crusade resulted in the death of many children along the way; the survivors suffered great hardship and were continually forced to beg food and warm clothes from the farmers they met in their travels.

In this extract, Simon (one of the crusaders) asks a farmer for food and water. Suddenly David, the farmer's son, says he wants to join Simon and the other children on their crusade. His father responds:

FARMER: (*The farmer collects the water and bag of food, and lays them at* SIMON'S *feet.*) Take these. Now you can have all that and what's in my barn. Take my jacket, you must be cold in the mountains. (*He takes it off.*) You can have all these. But leave me my son.

SIMON: Is that everything you have?

FARMER: That's everything I have.

SIMON: I respect your sacrifice. It speaks well of the love you have for your son . . .

FARMER: You say you are hungry . . . there's meat in there. A sack of grain. If you take him you will get nothing. Understand? No food, nothing. Less than nothing — you take on another mouth to feed. (*Pause.*) Now choose. My son or my goods?

SIMON: You have little understanding of our cause. First of all we are not going off to war, we go in peace to put an end to war. Secondly, we intend to make no compromises. We shall not repeat the mistakes our fathers made.

FARMER: Choose!

SIMON: The choice is very easy. Your son.
(*And this should be a difficult choice for Simon.*)

FARMER: Take him.

DAVID: I'm sorry, father.

FARMER: Go!

As you prepare to perform

This extract creates strong tension in a very short time.

Think about

As you prepare the scene you will need to consider the following questions.

1   What relationship exists between the farmer and his son? Devise a list of reasons why the farmer would not want David to go on the crusade. Why does David want to leave with Simon?

2   What tensions are operating on each of the three characters?

3   When does the moment of greatest tension occur in the extract?

4   How can you use movement and space between the characters to add to the tension?

5   How does David react to his father's final 'Go!', and how do the children leave the acting space?

Try out the scene

1   In groups of three read the scene two or three times. Decide who will be the farmer, Simon and David. Discuss the source of the dramatic tension in the scene, and the tensions affecting each character.

2   Set up your acting area and gather the props you need.

3 Focus

In any dramatic situation, where people and ideas meet, there are dozens of dramas waiting to happen. They can't all happen at once or they will muddle each other up, so we must decide to explore just one aspect of the situation. This is the playwright's focus. In this chapter we look at how the playwright or drama group focuses the action to make it dramatic.

Focusing the action

In our kind of drama the whole group is the playwright. A drama about the Olympic Games, for instance, could be focused on:
- choosing the relay team — what tensions does it put on the whole squad?
- cheating — should we use bodybuilding drugs, or tricks to 'psych out' the opponents?
- politics — should we compete with countries whose political system we condemn?
- commercialism — should we make a profit? What is a reasonable profit?

You may already have an interest in some aspect of the Olympics, and questions you would want a drama to answer. You will notice that the points of focus above have been framed as questions.

Be careful with your questions: you may have strong opinions on some aspect of the Olympics. Fine, go with them — but you shouldn't have all the answers already. If you set out to create a drama about wicked profiteers ripping off innocent athletes, you will probably end up with predictable situations and characters, and the drama will not be fresh or exciting. In the end it will be less convincing, because it tells you nothing you don't already know.

Activity 1

What focusing questions can you come up with for a drama about the Olympic Games, its participants and goals?
- what would happen if . . .?
- why did . . . happen?
- how could . . .?
- what is the most important . . .?
- why do (athletes/officials/terrorists, etc) . . .?

The drama could be between two or three people, or could include the whole group. You needn't even be bound by the size of your group — people can play different roles in different scenes.

Framing the action: an Olympics drama

Deciding your central question will limit which aspect of the subject, which bit of action, you will explore. The next issue is how best to explore it. The most obvious way is to get in and act it out, but there are other, maybe better, ways of doing it.

In a famous incident in the 1984 Olympic Games, the two favourites in the women's 3000 metres were Mary Decker, of the United States, and Zola Budd, a South African running for Great Britain. During the event, Budd apparently tripped Decker, putting her out of the race, which was eventually won by neither of them, but by a Rumanian, Maricica Puica. Read the newspaper account of the incident on page 36.

Let us suppose that you have decided to focus on this incident, to find out how and why such a thing could happen. (Remember, our drama is fiction: we will not necessarily find out anything about the real Budd and Decker. Instead, we will find out about characters who are like them, people in a similar position.) Where you start the drama depends on two things:
- what you and your drama space are capable of
- exactly what question you want to ask: and it may be necessary to refine your original question, as we shall see.

You could, obviously, re-enact the race. Try it, if you like.

From RON REED and AAP in Los Angeles

South African-born Zola Budd's controversial appearance at the Olympic Games ended in heartbreak and tears yesterday.

The day the tears flowed

The tiny, barefooted 18-year-old found herself cast as the villain of the Games after America's darling, Mary Decker, crashed out of the 3000 m final.

Budd was jeered and booed by sections of the 80,000 crowd at the Olympic Coliseum after a mid-race jostle which left Budd's left leg bleeding from spike marks and world champion Decker, who later accused Budd of knocking her out of the race, sprawled in agony on the inside of the track.

Rumanian Maricica Puica survived the jostling to run a superb race and take the gold medal in Olympic record time.

But, as Puica celebrated her victory, Decker was carried sobbing from the track by her fiance and taken to hospital for an X-ray and treatment to a pulled muscle at the top of her left leg.

Budd, who had always idolised the American, was also in tears, upset that she had been blamed for Decker's fall and by the fact that Decker had refused to speak to her when she approached the American in the athlete's tunnel after the race.

Budd, who had faded to finish seventh, then learned that she had been been disqualified for her race tactics. She was reinstated a few hours later following a protest by the British team management.

Decker was still sobbing when she told a news conference later: "I do hold Zola Budd responsible for what happened. It may be her inexperience but . . ."

Describing her fall, Decker said: "Someone cut in front of me and it was a matter of pushing her or me falling. When I went down I felt something in my left hip. I tried to get up but I couldn't. I wanted to get back into the race."

Puica said after the medals ceremony that she thought Decker was to blame: "It was Mary's fault. Mary was the girl behind and should have seen the way forward."

More reports, Page 2, Olympics liftout

THE SUNDAY MAIL, BRISBANE, AUSTRALIA 12.8.84

Activity 2

(. . . for the brave or foolish!)

1 Make the space you are working in like the Los Angeles stadium. Try to create the colour, the noise, the sense of enormous size and tiny figures. You might like to try it on the oval of a sports ground.

2 Keep your runners going for 3000 metres (for the tension of the race has to do with how long it takes, the ritual repetition of laps, the agony of the athletes).

3 Try to re-create, in the emptiness of the oval, the colour, excitement and passion of the cheering crowd of 100 000.

If you have been brave enough to try this, and even if you do manage it, what has it actually told you about your central question? Maybe *how* it happened. But certainly not much about *why*.

Activity 3

Now try one or more of the following scenes as an opening into the drama.
- In the changing room after the race, all the athletes are gathered, and Budd and Decker come face to face.
- Budd and Decker explain to their distressed parents what happened.
- Budd and Decker meet each other's parents.
- Budd faces a press conference.

You might like to get more information about the incident, to find out the kind of people these athletes are. Or you may prefer to decide these details for yourselves, as our drama is fiction.

You'll recall that in Chapter 1 we discussed the way that written activities help us document and understand our dramas. The next two activities include a documenting task which you will need as part of the dramatic activity. Writing is not the only medium for documenting, however, so in these activities we are expanding the field and working in other media.

Activity 4

The famous Budd — Decker race was 3000 metres long, lasted over 8½ minutes, and the final result was:
1. Maricica Puica (Rumania) 8min. 35.96 sec.
2. Wendy Sly (G. B.) 8min. 39.47 sec.
3. Lynn Williams (Can.) 8 min 42.14 sec.
4. Cindy Bremser (U. S.) 8 min. 42.73 sec.
5. Cornelia Buerki (Switz.) 8 min. 45.20 sec.
6. Aurora Cunta (Port.) 8 min. 46.37 sec.
7. Zola Budd (G. B.) 8 min. 48.80 sec.
8. Joan Hansen (U. S.) 8 min. 51.53 sec.
9. Dianne Rodger (N. Z.) 8 min. 56.43 sec.
10. Agnese-Possamai (Italy) 9 min. 10.82 sec.

Cont.

D.N.F. (Did not finish): Brigitte Kraus (W. Germ), Mary Decker (U.S.).

Working with one or two others, devise, briefly practise, and then record a radio commentary of your version of the whole race, including the notorious incident. Work to capture the atmosphere of the Olympics, the excitement of the race, and the catastrophe of the crash. Don't worry too much about the technical aspects of your recording; it doesn't need to be broadcast quality – just good enough for you to use as a prop.

Now, selecting one of the following contexts, run the commentary of the race, and respond to it in role as:

1 Budd's family and friends in South Africa.

2 A small portion of the crowd in the stadium, including:
    • patriotic Americans
    • patriotic Britons
    • a couple of white South Africans
    • a couple of black South African expatriates.

3 Neutral Australians in a club or pub at the time of the race.

Remember, you are just in role — you don't need to use accents.

Activity 5

In threes, take on the roles of a television sports crew covering the Olympics. In your threesome, decide which country you are from and agree together on a shared attitude you hold towards this Budd – Decker race.
You could choose to:

   • oppose South Africans taking part in the Olympics, especially when sheltered by another country's colours
   • sympathise with Budd as a victim of publicity
   • want to be scrupulously fair to all concerned
   • cynically see the incident as an opportunity for milking the audience's emotions.

Once you have done this, discuss in role how your newscrew will make the sixty second TV news broadcast telling your viewers what happened, and who is to blame.

If you have access to a portable TV camera and unit, video your broadcast. Again don't worry about technical quality. Concentrate on conveying your attitude about this event that has 'shaken the Olympics'.

If you are unable to video your broadcast you will be able to act it out live as if to the camera. When all your broadcasts have been prepared (and recorded if possible) play them back for the group, one after the other. Note the different attitudes of the TV crews . . . and the effect that this has on the 'truth'.

Choosing the dramatic frame

When and where we decide to set the action, we call the frame. Each of the preceding activities provided a strong starting point for action, even though each of them is some distance from the actual event, the race itself.

- In Activity 3, the scene focused on the main characters, but was after the event
- In Activity 4, the event is happening, but the characters are on the edge of it
- In Activity 5, both time and characters are outside the event.

All these approaches can build on dramatic tension, because the race, and the emotions it arouses, are still central to the action. Which frame you choose depends on what you want to explore — your exact question: the pressures on the athletes, the politics, the effect of publicity, etc.

We can show this in a diagram with our exercises as examples. The line of tension stretches away from the centre of the event, and it is that tension which keeps our interest. You can use this diagram to plan the focus of any dramatic situation, to help you 'frame the action'.

Framing the action

line of tension

Inside the event

On the edge of the event

Outside the event

And in plays . . .

Extract 4: from *The York Crucifixion Play* (anon, c1400)

Playwrights often focus the action away from the centre of the dramatic event, for many reasons. In ancient Greece, for example, violence and bloodshed were not thought to be suitable viewing. They always happened offstage, and the playwrights had to find the right character and the right moment to report them to the audience.

A little more recently, townspeople in the Middle Ages used to act out the whole history of Christianity on certain feast days. Everyone took part, making the whole day an exciting theatrical event. In York, the nailmakers (of all people!) were given the story of the Crucifixion to present. Imagine how difficult that must have been. How do you show the most momentous and symbolic event in Christian history, and make it meaningful and believable? Especially as the event itself was both violent and undignified.

The way the citizens of York solved the problem was by shifting the focus to the edge of the event. This was unexpected — instead of focusing on Jesus, they centred their action on the soldiers putting up the cross. This brought it home to their audience, for the soldiers are portrayed as very ordinary and contemporary working men; they joke and quarrel as they perform what is for them a run-of-the-mill, sweaty job.

The power of the play lies in the gap between what we know of the Crucifixion (the mighty event that changed the world), and what we see of it (blokes with hammers banging in nails and carelessly lashing ropes).

Jesus speaks occasionally, in words familiar to the audience: 'Lord, forgive them, for they know not what they do', but the soldiers hardly hear him: 'Lo,' they say, 'he chatters like a magpie'. But the audience hears, and is shocked — because *they can see themselves* in the performers.

3RD SOLDIER: I think we're ready, by and large.
Ya'd better do it right as rain.

4TH SOLDIER: This mug we've got in our charge
A long, long time 'e'll feel the pain.

1ST SOLDIER: OK then lads, now let's get working.

2ND SOLDIER: I've got 'is 'ands, see — I'm not shirking!

3RD SOLDIER: I'll drag 'em to the 'ole we've bored —
I don't think we'll need ropes and cord.

1ST SOLDIER: Well, pull yer 'ardest, then by Jeez!

2ND SOLDIER: 'Ere is a good and solid pin —
This nail should 'old 'is weight with ease.
We'll stick it right through bone and skin
No trouble — this job is a breeze!

1ST SOLDIER: 'Ang on a bit — what's up your way?
This business isn't over yet.

3RD SOLDIER: The 'ole's a foot or more astray!
'Is muscles are all shrunk, I bet.

4TH SOLDIER: I think the 'ole's bored out of true.

2ND SOLDIER: So? 'E can suffer a bit more.

3RD SOLDIER: Yeah, someone's bored it way askew,
It's nowhere near, and that's for sure.

1ST SOLDIER: Stop yakking — grab a piece of cord
And tug 'im over, top and toe.

3RD SOLDIER: 'Oo you ordering about, 'My Lord'?
Damn you, 'elp! Give us a go . . .

As you prepare to perform

The whole play continues in this vein; in fact some parts are even more gruesome than the extract quoted.

Think about

Some of you may have seen the film *Monty Python's Life of Brian*, which takes the idea of *The York Crucifixion Play* one frame further. It takes us through exactly the same events, but this time the hero is not Jesus at all. At the end of the film, the very ordinary people who are being crucified break into a silly, sentimental song, 'Always look on the bright side of life', which is such an unexpected contrast that the comic absurdity makes the event even more grotesque and excruciating. Interestingly, this film offended some people, while in the Middle Ages, a much more religious period than ours, people were able to take such a comic treatment completely in their stride.

Try out the scene

1 If you can, get hold of some ropes and hammers and blocks of timber.

2 Don't worry that the scene is in verse. We have translated it into modern language to help you. Make it sound as ordinary as you can, and make the soldiers realistic working men.

3 Try characterising the soldiers:
- 1st Soldier obviously thinks he's the foreman, and spends a lot of the play ordering the others around without getting his own hands dirty.
- 2nd Soldier is a bit of a sadist.
- 3rd Soldier is a cranky perfectionist.
- 4th Soldier is another sadist, but he's not very bright.

Focusing the dramatic moment

There is another aspect of focus which is important for the clarity and direction of your drama. Consider this account of a drama set up by some fourteen-year-olds.

'The class broke into three groups. One group was to be kids in a cafe, others decided to be bikers and all the rest became police. The bikers came into the cafe and immediately became a nuisance. They sat on tables and the counter, hassled all of the customers and started smashing

things. Someone called the police and they ran in and started arresting the bikers who fought back. Soon everyone was in it with kids yelling and wrestling and running everywhere. Jason got hurt when I stood on his hand.'

Obviously this attempt at drama was disastrous. For this group the drama became just an excuse for fooling around. You can probably spot at least three reasons why this drama went horribly wrong.

- There hadn't been any work done to develop roles or characters — should bikers and police automatically begin fighting? Don't police ride bikes too?
- There had been no attempt made to establish or develop tension — the action centred on empty conflict.
- No doubt you have also seen that the group lacked a clear frame for their drama.

Maintaining focus

There was another major weakness in that piece. The action was chaotic and no single moment was clear. The participants were scattered around the room, doing whatever they thought would be fun. Only when we focus each moment dramatically will the action have a clear centre and tension develop. As a drama progresses, a sharp focus must be maintained otherwise the action will become blurred and the direction lost.

The best dramatic action is made up of a series of focused moments and focused images. As creators of dramatic action you need techniques to ensure this happens. There are at least eight important ways participants can help maintain a sharp focus as the action advances. As you work through these you may discover more.

1 Space

A thoughtful use of space maintains focus. Levels (varying heights), physical proximity and groupings are all means of focusing action. When the Queen arrives in a foreign country for a State visit she will appear alone at the top of the aircraft steps, walk down the red carpet to the carefully arranged welcoming party, and pose for the photographers.

2 Places of special meaning

At times you will need to establish places of special meaning in your drama. Because all participants will understand the significance of such a place, any action which occurs there

will focus the drama. Such an area may be:
- the tribe's sacred land
- a monarch's chamber
- the gallows.

Activity 6

Remember the Olympic Games drama (p. 35): now you can prepare for the medal-giving ceremony.

Construct a winner's stand and select three people to be the medal winners: gold, silver and bronze. Choose somebody to present the medals; everyone else will be other officials, athletes, coaches, etc.
- How many officials will you need to make the scene look authentic and impressive? Where will they stand?
- Decide exactly where everyone will be in order to keep the focus on the ceremony and the winner's stand.

Note your positions, as we will develop this activity further.

3   Established patterns

Dramatic action will often provide opportunities for characters to create things to do which can be repeated regularly throughout the drama. For example:
- at the factory, repetitive mime sequences can represent work tasks
- a primitive tribe can develop a ritual chant in praise of their volcano.

Once these patterns have been established, each time the characters return to them, a clear focus for the action is ensured.

Activity 7

Back at the medals ceremony, return to the positions you had taken up. Establish the exact sequence of words and movement for the giving of each medal. Practise the ceremony once or twice, until it looks imposing.

If you wish to use appropriate music and applause this will add to the scene.

4 Properties

'Properties' (props) are items essential to the dramatic action. When props are introduced they often serve to focus the drama. For example:

- a key ('This is the key to the treasury, it never leaves my side!')
- a diary ('I must hide this from my boyfriend!')
- a letter ('So you have it! Give it back this instant').

Activity 8

Obviously, in the medals ceremony, the medals themselves, with their ribbons, are vital props. You will need to find or make something to represent them.

- Are they resting on a cushion, or a tray, or in a box?
- What would you be wearing — think particularly of the colours?

With the props, and costumes if you wish, repeat the ceremony.

5 Gesture

Any gesture which concentrates attention (eg pointing, facing the action, touching) also helps to establish focus more clearly.

Activity 9

Now concentrate on the gestures of the three winners. How do you ensure that the focus remains on each of them at the vital moment?

- Are family or friends in the crowd? Are the winners proud for their country?
- When and how do they congratulate the others?

All class members should make suggestions for the three medallists to try out, to help each of them achieve the most effective gestures.

6 Eye contact

When teachers say 'Look here everyone', they are securing the focus of attention in the room by insisting that everybody looks at the same thing. Just as in real life, eye contact between individuals and within groups is an important way of controlling and focusing the action.

Activity 10

Act out the whole scene again incorporating the special gestures of the medal winners. At each key moment all eyes will be on those gestures, enjoying their triumph — that's obvious enough. However, during the scene each character will also have other interesting or startling things to look at; will observe and make meaningful glances, etc. How can these add to the dramatic atmosphere? Experiment, but at all times keep the focus of interest clear, especially during those key moments.

7 Language and voice

In most dramatic action the person speaking is normally the centre of attention, the focus. However, focus is determined not just by who is speaking, but also by what is being said and the way it is being said. For example, the person speaking the most loudly is often the centre of focus.

Activity 11

Now to refine the language and voice in our Olympic Games scene. This will involve planning and perhaps even scripting, because it is a very formal occasion. You will need to decide:
- the loudspeaker announcements
- the formal congratulations by the presenter, and perhaps an informal comment too
- what the medallist replies, and how
- what the others say to each other, how and when.

Now experiment with the sound levels. The loudspeaker will of course be loud and easily command focus. You may care to use a real microphone — and see what effect that has. On the other hand, one of the medallists may be almost inaudible, but all ears will be straining to hear her.

How is the general hubbub managed around these strong focuses?

8 Contrasts

Focus is also achieved through contrasting images, for example when:
- all players are moving quickly — except one who is still
- all players are chanting softly — except one who speaks above the chant
- all players are in darkness — except one who is in the light.

The use of contrast is particularly effective and incorporates a number of the focusing techniques discussed earlier.

Activity 12

We have set the scene of Puica's glorious triumph, but where are Budd and Decker? They certainly won't be sharing the glory, though they are probably in the crowd.

1 Choose two of the other athletes to be Budd and Decker, who will now become the real centre of focus. All their actions will be in stark contrast to what has already been created.

2 As a class, plan these contrasts, referring to the seven ways of maintaining focus we have already listed.

- **Space**: How close are Budd and Decker to the other athletes? How close to each other? Which way are they facing?
- **Place of special meaning**: Should they be near the medals stand?
- **Established patterns**: As each medal is presented, what do they do?
- **Props**: Can any prop emphasise their distress? Might any item of costume pick them out from the crowd?
- **Gesture**: What special gestures might they use?
- **Eye contact**: Do they look at the medals? Do they look at each other? Who looks at them? When?
- **Voice and language**: Do they say anything? To whom? How?

3 Now try the scene one last time. Believe in what you are doing and it will be powerful, because it is now clearly focused and complete.

And in plays . . .

Extract 5: from *Oh What a Lovely War* by Joan Littlewood's Theatre Workshop

In any good play or scene the action is clearly focused. The following extract shows the very clever effect that can be created by sudden changes of focus. *Oh What a Lovely War* is a play telling the story of World War 1, using the songs the soldiers sang in the trenches. This episode, a parody of a front-line church service, sets the scene for the slaughters of the Battle of Arras. Like *The York Crucifixion Play*, it uses comedy to highlight the horror.

(*Haig, a chaplain, a nurse and soldiers come on.*)

CHAPLAIN: Let us pray.

All sing. The soldiers sing their own version of the hymns. The chaplain, Haig, and the nurse sing the correct words.

SONG: FORWARD JOE SOAP'S ARMY
            (*Tune: 'Onward Christian Soldiers'*)
Forward Joe Soap's army, marching without fear,
With our old commander, safely in the rear.
He boasts and skites from morn till night,
And thinks he's very brave,
But the men who really did the job are dead and in
            their grave.
Forward Joe Soap's army, marching without fear,
With our old commander, safely in the rear.
Amen.

. . .

CHAPLAIN: Let us pray. O God, show thy face to us as thou didst with thy angel at Mons. The choir will now sing 'What a friend we have in Jesus' as we offer a silent prayer for Sir Douglas Haig for success in tomorrow's onset.

SONG: WHEN THIS LOUSY WAR IS OVER
            (*Tune: 'What a friend we have in Jesus'*)

When this lousy war is over,
No more soldiering for me,
When I get my civvy clothes on,

Oh, how happy I shall be!
No more church parades on Sunday,
No more putting in for leave,
I shall kiss the sergeant-major,
How I'll miss him, how he'll grieve!
Amen.

CHAPLAIN: O Lord, now lettest thou thy servant depart in peace, according to thy word. Dismiss.

CORPORAL (*blowing a whistle*):   Come on, you men, fall in.

(*The soldiers sing as they march off.*)

• • •

CHAPLAIN: Land of our birth, we pledge to thee, our love and toil in the years to be.

HAIG: Well, God, the prospects for a successful attack are now ideal. I place myself in thy hands.

CHAPLAIN: Into thy hands I commend my spirit.

NURSE: The fields are full of tents, O Lord, all empty except for as yet unmade and naked iron bedsteads. Every ward has been cleared to make way for the wounded that will be arriving when the big push comes.

HAIG: I trust you will understand, Lord, that as a British gentleman I could not subordinate myself to the ambitions of a junior foreign commander, as the politicians suggested. It is for the prestige of my King and Empire, Lord.

CHAPLAIN: Teach us to rule ourself alway, controlled and cleanly night and day.

HAIG: I ask thee for victory, Lord, before the Americans arrive.

NURSE: The doctors say there will be enormous numbers of dead and wounded, God.

CHAPLAIN: That we may bring if need arise, no maimed or worthless sacrifice.

HAIG: Thus to grant us fair weather for tomorrow's attack, that we may drive the enemy into the sea.

NURSE: O Lord, I beg you, do not let this dreadful war cause all the suffering that we have prepared for. I know you will answer my prayer.

(*Explosion. They go off.*)

As you prepare to perform

Think about

Notice how, when the two versions of the songs are being sung, the focus is deliberately split and confused. Then when the soldiers have gone off, the focus becomes clear, and switches quickly among the three isolated kneeling figures. The sudden jumps, from the pious platitudes of the chaplain, to the smug arrogance of Haig, to the sincere anguish of the nurse, all add to the telling contrast.

Note too that in this section, the chaplain, the nurse and Haig are all continuing their speeches as if they were speaking alone. If you read only the chaplain's lines, one after the other, you will see that they are in verse, and should be spoken that way.

Try out the scene

Play this scene as a whole class. Set it up as if in church, with the soldiers standing very smartly (though some of them might be wounded). The chaplain, the nurse and Haig (British Commander-in-Chief) should be well apart from each other.

Some of you will probably know the tunes of the songs. Try to get hold of the original words and music. The key characters should be singing the correct words while the soldiers are singing their own versions. The better the songs are sung, the more powerful the scene will be. Play it very straight and let the humour do its own work.

4 Place and space

All dramatic action occurs in time and space. Playwrights need to choose the place where they set the action carefully, as setting can greatly affect the events and tensions within the drama. While *Star Wars* rages across galaxies in many colourful locations, *Hamlet* is mainly set in a dreary, claustrophobic castle . . .

The place

Suppose you create a drama called *Leaving Home* to explore the love/hate relationship between a girl and her father which leads to the girl leaving home. What differences would there be if you set the action:
- in a one-parent home
- in a transit camp for refugees
- in an expensive boarding school where father and daughter seldom meet, though they often write?

How you intend to frame the action is, of course, clearly connected to your setting. Remember our Olympic Games saga: if you had the resources to make a film, the stadium could be a very powerful location — as it is in the films *Chariots of Fire* and *Ben Hur*. But for the confrontation scene between Zola and Mary, the confined, sweaty, crowded dressing room is far more apt.

Activity 1

1 Take the idea for the *Leaving Home* drama and, as a class, choose one of the three suggested settings (or make up another if you prefer).

2 Divide into three groups, and referring to the 'Framing the action' diagram on page 39, each group choose one frame.

3 See if each group can frame a scene about the father/daughter relationship, choosing the most appropriate setting for it.
- **Inside the event**: Where would you set a scene in which the two of them row about her boyfriend?
- **On the edge**: Where would you set a scene where the girl is confiding to a friend about her problems with her father?
- **Outside the event**: Where would you set a scene in which neighbourhood gossips discuss the girl's departure?

Aspects of place

Different settings will dictate which other characters might be introduced; certain settings will intensify the action, while the use of contrasting settings can help to build the dramatic tension. There are four aspects of place that you should keep in mind when choosing the best setting for each scene, and for the drama as a whole.

1 Other characters

Your setting may limit, or dictate, the range of other characters you can use in your drama. It may also suggest minor characters you can bring in. For example, if you set *Leaving Home* in:
- a one-parent home — you could include kindly or interfering neighbours.

- a refugee camp — you could bring in an unsympathetic camp official.
- the school yard — laughing or embarrassed schoolmates could crowd around and intensify the action.

Activity 2

Go back to your three groups. Look again at your setting to see which other people are likely to be around. Choose one or more who might have a significant effect on the way the action develops, and re-enact the scene incorporating these new roles.

2   Closed and open settings

As we have mentioned, *Hamlet* is mainly set in a closed, gloomy castle, which intensifies the fears, the hates and the struggle for power. Not all dramas are so intense, and a more open and spacious setting may allow more variety in the action. In a drama about Robin Hood, for example, the villagers would have their separate homes, their trades and their family concerns.

Multiple locations enable us to explore many aspects of the situation. One scene could be set in the village, another in Robin's hideout, and a third in King Richard's tent in the

Holy Land, as he refuses to be bothered with local matters back in England.

The more open the location, the more chance there is of the outside world affecting the action. Medieval villagers have visitors, go on pilgrimages, face outbreaks of plague. On the other hand, to take an extreme example, in a nuclear fallout shelter the characters are entirely on their own.

Some dramas lend themselves to either approach: a drama on the Russian revolution could span a continent, or it could all be set in one cell in the Lubyanka prison. The choice is yours.

Activity
3

Go back to your scene, see how open or closed the setting is, and experiment with setting it at the other end of the scale. Does it work more effectively, or not so well?

3   Contrasting settings

Films often use contrast between closed and open locations to help establish mood and meaning. In *Crocodile Dundee*, for instance, even the characters are defined by their location. The first part, Dundee's territory, is wide Australian outback. This section is shot with a background of broad expanses, great trees and rocks, vast, peaceful waters, while the humans are solitary, small figures. The township is deserted, and even the sprawling pub is half-empty.

As soon as the story shifts to New York city, the screen is perpetually crowded with people, especially in the frantic bustle of the streets. The bars here are tiny and jammed to the doors. Why do you think the final scene, where the 'outback hero gets his girl against all odds', is set where it is — after all, it would be difficult to imagine a more spectacularly closed and cramped location!

Other classic films which make powerful use of the contrast between closed and open settings include *My Brilliant Career*, *Witness*, and almost any Hitchcock thriller.

4   Messages of place

Many settings carry with them very strong *associations*: things which we expect to happen in that place. Our expectations of a prison cell, for instance, are different from those of a Christmas party, and these associations will add to your drama. You can also contrast expectations powerfully. This sets up a tension of surprise between what we expect and what is actually happening: a group of underground revolutionaries using a church as their meeting place, for instance.

Activity
4

Go back again to your scene, and try setting it in a place which is quite unexpected, for example, in *Leaving Home* the row might happen at a Christmas party. By now you have probably developed the outline of the scene. Improvise it again, and let the setting have its impact on the characters.

The space

Once you have decided on a location for your drama, consider how your drama space (the room or hall you're working in) can be arranged. With just a few resources and a large enough space, you can create a good, workable studio. Setting your space up thoughtfully can give you a lot more scope and make your dramas much stronger.

Creating a drama studio

Rostra blocks (strong boxes of different shapes, sizes and heights) help you create different levels. If you can't get these, strong tables, desks and chairs will do. Sheets or lengths of hessian will have many uses: they can be spread out to mark territory, or suspended to form walls. It is also a great help if you can black out your space. This will give you much more flexibility. You should also be able to play audio tapes or records. In all, your drama space must be a flexible working area, and you need to feel free to arrange it to suit your purposes.

Arranging the space

When you have decided the setting for your drama, consider how best to set up your drama space to create that location.

- How much space should be allocated to create that setting? If the action is set in an aeroplane, you could limit the space to the real dimensions of an aircraft.
- What does the setting dictate about the organisation of space? In a waiting room, for example, chairs are often arranged back to back; in an aircraft, they are separated by an aisle.
- Does the drama need a large space for a whole-group activity to focus the group? A tribal drama might use a large meeting place.
- Would the use of different levels help focus the action or suggest power? A drama set on a ship could use levels to distinguish the bridge from the engine room.
- Do you need a section of the room which cannot be observed for moments of secrecy and privacy?
- How much space separates areas? What about private areas — can people overhear what happens in private settings?
- Do all participants have access to all of the spaces? Which areas are high status — the boss's office, the throne-room?

Activity
5

1   Break into four groups: **A,B,C** and **D**

2   Groups **A** and **B** are each to design a setting for a drama set in a nuclear fallout shelter after a nuclear attack. All class members are to be catered for in the shelter.

3   Groups **C** and **D** are each to design a setting for 'Asgard', the home of the gods in Norse mythology. Asgard was

depicted as an enormous enclosure with individual dwellings for the lords who lived there. Full of fabulous riches, it was built of splendid materials, which were particularly handsome in the great council and banquet hall, the 'Halle'.

4 Each group is to design its own setting. Discuss what possibilities your space offers before you commit your ideas to paper. (A sketch with notes will be sufficient.)

5 Groups **A** and **B** are to set up their nuclear shelters in the space, and explain to the rest of the class why they made the decisions they did. Similarities and differences in the two designs should be noted: which setting has the richest possibilities for action? Why?

6 Repeat this process with Groups **C** and **D**, this time comparing the two Asgards.

And in plays . . .

Extract 6: from *The Fourth Year Are Animals*

Back in the high school we first encountered in Chapter 1, Alan Howman has been trying to find something to interest the fourth year 'animals', as they are affectionately called by his colleague, Marie. He takes Marie's advice that . . . "some of the best lessons come from late night TV. 4F will all be watching it so why shouldn't you?" As part of a sequence of ill-fated lessons based on *The Curse of The Mummy's Tomb* he takes them on a trip to the museum. As well as Kelly, her sidekick Theresa and the simple-minded Arthur are part of the class.

> (*The children mill around as* ALAN, *armed with his book on Egypt, points out the delights of the exhibition.*)

ALAN: (*reads*) 'The eyes of the body have been removed and replaced with enamel eyes. The embalmer's next task was to remove the brain via the nostrils with a curved instrument . . .'

> (*Kelly sticks a crooked finger up her nose.*)

KELLY: Like this, Sir?

> (*THERESA groans,* KELLY *goes and leans on the glass case.*)

ALAN: 'Many mummies have been found wearing rings and other jewellery'.

KELLY: My mummy does that.

(ALAN *notices that she is leaning on the glass.*)

ALAN: Kelly, what does it say on that sign?

KELLY: (*reads*) 'Please do not lean on glass.' Oh, *this* glass, Sir.

(*She moves away from the case.* ARTHUR *immediately takes her place leaning on the glass.*)

ALAN: Now there's still a few minutes left before the bus comes. You may just wander about and look at whatever you like but stay on this floor and don't touch!

(ARTHUR *moves away from the glass.* KELLY *and* THERESA *sneak off for a quiet smoke.*)

Those who've finished their question sheets can hand them in to me now. What is it, Arthur?

ARTHUR: (*Pointing to the glass case*) What are all those cockroaches for, Sir?

ALAN: What cockroaches?

ARTHUR: There Sir — under the glass.

ALAN: Oh no, Arthur — they're scarab beetles. They had a sort of religious meaning for the Egyptians.

ARTHUR: Why are they shrivelled up, Sir?

ALAN: They're over four thousand years old.

THERESA: (*as* KELLY *puts a cigarette in her mouth*)   Oh come on, give us one.

KELLY: It'll make too much smoke. He'll see.

ARTHUR: Are they dead ones, Sir?

ALAN: I expect they are, Arthur.

THERESA: Oh go on.

KELLY: I'll give you a puff of mine, OK?

THERESA: I paid for half of them!

KELLY: Sshh!

(ALAN *has heard this and crosses to them.*)

ALAN: Ahem!

(*They look up guiltily.* KELLY *still holds an unlighted cigarette in her mouth.* THERESA *sidles off.*)

As you prepare to perform

In this scene we are concentrating on the use of place and space. The roles and relationships we already know, basically, from the scene we looked at in Chapter 1. Now we are looking at how they are affected by the messages of the place.

Think about

Place

The scene is a lesson, set in a museum, not a classroom. The messages are different, and so is what we expect to happen there. What differences are there in:
- atmosphere
- noise levels
- furniture and the amount of open space?

You can probably tell that Alan is having difficulty with this class, even in their normal environment.
- How do these differences in place add to his difficulties?
- How do they add to the tension and humour of the action?

Space

You can emphasise the tension and humour in the action by careful management of your space. You will need quite a large floor space to represent a museum.
- Is it empty, vast and echoing, apart from the glass case indicated in the text?
- Is it crowded with cases and corners of cases everywhere?

Try out the scene

Either extreme of empty or crowded can be very effective, more so than the 'medium' clutter of a classroom. Either way, Alan has a problem. Your available space may suit one of these approaches better. If you can, try the scene both ways, and see which seems more effective in highlighting Alan's problems.
- Kelly and Theresa might sneak off to a far corner, where Alan has difficulty finding them among all the screens and cases.
- Alternatively, they might go for their smoke behind the very case full of 'cockroaches'.

Whatever you decide, the scene should emerge as a nightmare for Alan (it gets worse for him later on!). Remember, it must also be believable for the audience.

5 Time

If you look at any photograph, picture or sculpture of a group of people, you see their relationships in a moment frozen for ever. The moment raises questions.

- Who are they and what are they to each other?
- Why are they together — what has brought them to this moment?
- What happens afterwards?

Bring that moment to life and we have drama.

Narrative

We can explore the people and their story to answer the questions above. There is one other very important question: how does their story matter to us? Almost all drama and theatre is made up of a story or narrative. The events in a narrative are not random, but linked in sequence by cause and effect: this action happens because *these* people are in *this* context with *these* motives.

Activity 1

1   Look inside the front cover at Goya's *The Third of May*: the people are obviously not there by accident. See what it tells you about that moment — the event itself. Think about the questions at the beginning of this chapter. Look at the gestures, the costumes, the use of space, the expressions (why can't we see the soldiers' expressions?) Whose side are you on?

2   There is a story behind this painting. Make a list of the questions which you need to ask to find out that story. Perhaps start with asking who the victims are.

3   Now use group members to set up the picture physically as a frozen tableau as accurately as you can. Don't move or enact it yet. The rest of the group look at it, move round it to

gain a three-dimensional view, and see if there is any further information you need. For instance what expressions might the soldiers have? Ask the tableau group to try a few, and see what questions arise from those.

Time in action: the Goya drama

We will now bring this picture to life as a drama in five scenes, *The Goya Drama*. The questions you have asked will be the starting point for framing the action. The picture, and your tableau, are focused right in the event. We shall use other frames to make the story a dramatic journey through time. Our drama will explore why it happened and what it led to.

Exploring causes

To make this a historically based drama you will need to know more of the background of the picture.
- In 1808 the Emperor Napoleon of France seizes the throne of Spain.
- 2nd May 1808: in the capital, Madrid, rebellious Spaniards, afraid for the life of their young prince, riot against French troops. Many on both sides are killed.
- 3rd May 1808: in reprisal, French soldiers are ordered to execute all Spaniards believed to be in any way connected with the uprising.

Scene 1

Marching orders	
Date:	2nd May 1808
Setting:	The family quarters of the French soldiers in Perpignan, a town in France near the Spanish border.
Roles:	One quarter of the class are French soldiers, the others are their families.
Design:	Each family sets up its own space to ensure some privacy. Each house has a door on to the town square — keep one section of the space clear for this.

Cont.

Context: The soldiers have just been given orders to march for Spain; their families are helping them to prepare their equipment before they take their leave.

Constraints: 1 Everyone knows that war with Spain is imminent — this may be it!

2 The barracks is alight with rumours of a massacre of French troops by a Spanish mob in Madrid.

Management: 1 Divide into groups of three to five, each with one 'soldier'. Decide what your family relationship to the soldier is.

2 Look again at the picture to see exactly what equipment the soldiers will have, and decide who will do what job — sharpening the sabres, polishing the boots, etc.

3 Improvise this scene, miming the handling of equipment with care. Each soldier's life depends on his weapons, his boots, etc. Allow the scene to develop *slowly*, don't let it become a flippant comedy — if you wonder why, look again at the picture.

Outcomes: 1 After the Commanding Officer (the teacher or one of the 'troopers') has given the signal, they say their goodbyes, form up in the square and march away.

2 When this action has finished:
• *Soldiers* stay in role, and write the entry for that night in your diary (the diary that is important to you because a soldier's life is precarious). Describe your leave-taking, and perhaps ponder what is in store for you. If possible, you should do this immediately.
• *Family members*, do not stay in role, but start a journal of this drama — documenting what happened and your own feelings about the drama so far. You may have positive suggestions or critical comments to make, and may prefer to let a little time pass after the drama before you write it up.

Scene 2

First meeting

Date:	3rd May 1808, afternoon.
Setting:	The market place at Viure, a Spanish village just over the border, a day's march from Perpignan.
Roles:	The French soldiers as before. Choose one of the soldiers to be a drummer. Those who were families change role to become the Spanish inhabitants of Viure: shoppers, market stallholders. You can be the same age and sex as before. Choose one villager to be a bill poster.
Context:	The soldiers are camping near Viure. They have been sent into the village with French banknotes to buy supplies for the regiment.
Props:	**1** A drum — a snare drum if possible.
	2 Something to represent banknotes of the Banque National de France.
	3 A newsbill, made in advance as shown.

EXTRA

* BRUTAL FRENCH TROOPS SLAUGHTER UNARMED CITIZENS IN MADRID DEMONSTRATIONS

* FRENCH SOLDIERS PAY FOR THE CRIME WITH THEIR LIVES

* DEMONSTRATIONS EXPRESS FEAR FOR LIFE OF SPAIN'S INFANT PRINCE STILL MISSING

Constraints:	**1** The soldiers remember the rumours of savage Spanish rioters, but they are under strict orders not to get involved in any confrontation, on pain of court martial.

Cont.

2 The villagers have heard that the French are on their way to fight the Portuguese, Spain's enemy. They are used to French people, and have not yet heard of the riot in Madrid. The troops are colourful and an interesting change, and the villagers have a range of attitudes to them, from liking and admiration to mild distrust.

3 Living near the border, most of the Spanish speak French, though there may be a few who do not. Use English for both languages, of course.

4 The action of this scene should be brisk, full of the colour and movement of the market place and the soldiers' arrival.

5 There will be a change of mood during the scene, when a newsbill is posted.

Management: **1** Set up the market place with its stalls. The villagers should establish their roles in the market place, while the soldiers in their camp discuss what has happened to them since they left Perpignan.

2 Improvise the scene, starting with the locals haggling and swapping yarns. A distant drum is heard, and a little while later the soldiers march in to the brisk beat of the drummer. When the moment is right (*not too soon*) the bill poster puts up the newsbill, and calls the villagers' attention to it.

3 None of the French soldiers can read the notice — it is in Spanish. They are puzzled at the villagers' change of mood towards them.

Outcomes: **1** The soldiers get their supplies in the end.
2 When the action has finished:
- *Soldiers* write an entry in your diary, the account of this puzzling and perhaps unnerving event, that has just happened in the market place of Viure.
- *Villagers* again come out of role, and write your personal journal account of the drama today.

Exploring effects

Some of the questions you raised about the picture have probably been answered by these scenes. You now know more about the people involved. You will also be picking up some clues about the **causes** of the execution. As the drama moves through time, we can go on beyond the execution to explore its **effects**.

Now, to add some more background (fictional, this time). Some of you will probably be expecting this.

- The soldiers in our drama are the soldiers in the painting.
- The central victim in the painting, with arms outstretched, is a prominent and popular citizen of Viure. His name is Pepe Hermano (Hermano means 'brother').

Scene 3

	Aftermath
Date:	3rd May 1808, evening.
Setting:	The soldiers are back at their camp outside the village. The villagers are in the market square.
Context:	For the soldiers it is the first chance to talk with your comrades about the execution. For the villagers, news has just come through of the death of Pepe and many others.
Constraints:	Both groups should avoid extravagant displays of emotion — as you talk, the feelings will emerge.
Management:	Set this scene up simply, just separating the soldiers' space from the villagers'. Take another look at the picture and then improvise the scenes simultaneously.
Outcomes:	1 After you have talked over what happened, and found out how the others feel, conclude the scene.

2 *Soldiers:* writing the next diary entry is very important after this scene: when facing such powerful events, you may find that you can express yourself better in writing than in conversation.
Villagers: equally important are your impressions of this scene, and how the drama is going so far. |

And now some further historical background: the executions of the third of May sparked off a full-scale war, with the British under Wellington joining the Spanish rebels. It has been a brutal war, with atrocities on both sides. The British have been gaining ground, and now the Spanish towns are no longer safe for French soldiers. The French army is in full-scale retreat, in disarray, with many wounded.

Scene 4

Monument to the fallen

Date: 2 years later.

Setting: The market place in Viure.

Context: *Soldiers:* retreating in defeat, you are on your way home. Today, your regiment will struggle through Viure.
Villagers: the war has been hard on you too, but you have not forgotten your first martyr, Pepe Hermano. You have erected a monument to him and to your country's dead. Today is the unveiling.

Constraints: The soldiers will need help — food, water and medical care — but they are no longer in a position to demand anything.
For the villagers, the unveiling ceremony needs to be powerful. Remember the event it commemorates.

Management: 1 Make a simple monument to Pepe.

2 Set up the market again, as in scene 2, and place the monument, ready to be unveiled, in a prominent, open place.

3 In a separate space, the tired soldiers halt outside Viure for a while.

4 The villagers devise their unveiling ceremony. Decide who will officiate, and decide the order of ceremony. You may wish to include music, prayers, speeches, etc.

5 Meanwhile, the soldiers are writing letters home to France and talking among themselves. One may want to dwell on the bloodshed, on a friend's heroism, or his

own, or may just look forward to being home soon.

6 After these preparations, the scene starts with the ceremony. Just as the monument is unveiled, the soldiers struggle in, in twos and threes . . .

Outcome:

1 You may wish to plan the ending of this scene in advance, or wait and see what happens as you enact it.
2 When the action has finished:
  - *Soldiers:* write a final entry in your diary, the last entry of this awful war.
  - *Villagers:* as usual, come out of role, write your impressions of this scene, and sum up this dramatic narrative as a whole. (There will be one more scene, but quite different.)

Documenting and reflecting

At the end of each scene so far, we have asked you to make a diary entry — for some of you it was *inside* the drama, for some *outside*. For all of you it was *private*, a personal account of your own feelings and points of view. Both those who played soldiers and those who played villagers could equally usefully use the other approach — the soldiers writing from outside, the villagers from inside.

This is a very important aspect of documenting drama. Whether we are spectators at a theatre, or participants in an improvisation, for any drama to work, we need to feel strongly about what is happening. But we also need to think about the action, to reflect on what is happening, both in the drama and to ourselves. Writing allows us not only to fix our feelings, but to give them some distance. Tomorrow we will come to the drama cold and our sense of proportion will be different. Then, we can look back, through the writing, at the drama, and ask what the meaning was, and is.

After the final scene, you might like to devise your own documenting task or tasks.

The last scene in our Goya drama, explores how narrative is capable of making huge jumps in time without the drama falling apart. The scene illustrates how the effects of one moment can echo down through the ages.

Scene 5

Goya's Revenge

Date: The present day.

Setting: The Louvre, in Paris, one of the largest art galleries in the world.

Roles: **1** The French soldiers change role and become security guards at the Louvre.

     2 Of the others, half become tourists at the Louvre.

     3 The rest become modern Spanish patriots known as the 'Brotherhood of Pepe Hermano', prepared to do anything for their country.

Context: Our Goya drama has taken a major time jump. The Spanish Government has just given the painting *The Third of May* to France as a gesture of friendship between the two nations. The painting is given pride of place in the Louvre. Today is the first day of public viewing.

Constraints: **1** The patriots are committed to keeping the Goya in Spanish hands. They intend stealing the painting from the Louvre and holding it until they secure a guarantee that the painting will stay in Spain.

     2 The guards are responsible for the security of over 400 000 works of art. They are short staffed, and are not aware of an imminent attempt to steal the Goya.

     3 The tourists are enjoying a day at the gallery, excited to see the Goya for the first time. They also are unaware of any plans to steal the painting.

Design: Design the art gallery and locate the painting prominently. Make a plan of the gallery's security systems. Then, the patriots should plan how to carry out the theft of their national treasure.

Management: The action of this scene should be brisk and tight, especially during the theft of the painting. Feel free to rehearse the scene a couple of times to be completely sure of the action.

Outcome: **1** You may wish to play this scene more than once with different outcomes.
- The patriots manage to steal the painting, largely through cunning.
- The patriots steal the painting through force.
- The theft is foiled — the French keep the painting. What happens to the patriots?
- You could allow the outcome to unfold as you improvise.

2 Decide on your documenting task. As this scene is set in the present, it could be something for radio or television, instead of writing.

Time in perspective

We set the final scene in the present to illustrate the main purpose of a drama set in a historical time or faraway place. Drama can help us to understand how and why people behave the way they do today; can demonstrate that historical processes still have power over us. This is why people still find the plays of the ancient Greeks and Shakespeare moving and meaningful. You may have noticed that the action of the last scene, though set today, was quite similar to the scenes set in 1808. It too, was about patriotism, duty and rebellion, and rivalry between two countries.

Our Goya drama can give us insights into other matters that concern us today:
- today's wars and rebellions
- how people become victims or rebels
- whether the people who carry out repressive orders are really the villains or victims.

Aspects of time

There are many ways to 'play' with time to bring a drama to life — some of these we have already used in *The Goya Drama*. As with place there are some other aspects of time which we need to consider.

Closed and open time frames

For clear focus, some plays and dramas restrict themselves to brief periods. A performance of *Who's Afraid of Virginia Woolf* by Edward Albee lasts over three hours, is set in a single room, and the action all happens on one night between 2 am and dawn. *The Goya Drama* used a larger canvas, and jumped two centuries to show the long-term effects of an event.

We can take any liberties we like with time. Our drama started with the event — the execution — then used flashbacks (scenes 1 and 2) to explore the causes. To start the drama, we froze time in a tableau, rather than playing out the whole event. We made jumps of one day, two days, two years, and nearly two hundred years.

Messages of period

Just as each place brings strong associations and imposes constraints on your drama, so does the time period. If you are free to decide when to set your drama, you need to consider which period will be most apt for your theme, and will enrich it most.

Associations of period

Consider the associations of the period: a drama about law and order (good laws and bad laws) might well be enriched by setting it in the 1920s in Chicago, with its associations of gangsters and bootlegging. A drama about capital punishment would be powerfully enhanced by being set in 18th century London, in the shadow of Tyburn Gallows.

Constraints of period

When you have decided your period your dramatic action will be constrained by two things:
- *The levels of technology which existed*: Captain Cook cannot telephone London to announce his discovery of Australia, but must wait a year to break the news.
- *Social and economic conditions*: in the Middle Ages, working people were not allowed to travel without special permission, and had no money to speak of anyway, so few people ever left their village, and a traveller was a wonder.

Be prepared to do some research!

Tempo and timing

There is another aspect of time in drama: the actual time we spend doing an improvisation. When we improvise, the action takes place in *real time*, in seconds, minutes, perhaps even hours — in school, the length of a lesson. For this kind of time management we use the words tempo and timing.

Tempo

The tempo of a drama relates to the kind of action going on, and to the mood. A fight, for instance, will certainly proceed at a faster tempo than a funeral. A fast tempo demands sharp, energetic movements and speech, while a slow tempo is characterised by deliberate, controlled movement and speech.

Your drama used a range of tempos. In each case the tempo was dictated by the purpose of the scene.

Activity 2

With *The Goya Drama* in mind, reflect on the following questions regarding tempo.

1 What tempo was established for the first scene, the preparation and departure for war? Were there frequent pauses? How quickly did you pack and prepare your equipment? Did you move quickly or slowly when commanded to line up in the square?

2 Discuss the tempo which was established in each of the other four improvised scenes. Which scene moved most quickly? Which most slowly? Why?

3 Discuss the particular differences which occurred between the three scenes set in the market of Viure.

4 Was there ever a change of tempo within the one scene? In scene 5 for example, did the tempo increase once the theft took place?

Timing

Tempo refers to the management of time in a broad sense. The precise use of time, from one moment to the next, we call timing. It is an important factor in building dramatic tension — through long pauses or hasty interruptions, for example.

Activity 3

Consider these aspects of timing in *The Goya Drama*.

1 List the longest moment of silence you experienced in each scene.

2 Think back to times in the improvisations when it was necessary for you or others to speak quickly. Did this increase dramatic tension?

3 Do you recall moments when the timing needed to be handled differently? Were there moments when people spoke too quickly? Too slowly? Did not allow for silence? Held silences too long?

4 How was timing important in creating the most powerful moments in the drama? What about the moment that the bill poster chose to put up the newsbill in scene 2?

And in plays . . .

Extract 7: from *King John*
by William Shakespeare

Cause and effect follow swiftly on each other during this play: King Richard the Lionheart has died. His caretaker during the Crusades, King John, is now fighting the King of France for the throne of England. The French King wants the boy Prince Arthur to rule. After several battles, Arthur is captured by King John. John has a dilemma: the boy is a sweet, innocent lad, but he will always be a threat, even in prison. John impulsively speaks to the Knight, Sir Hubert, who has charge of the royal prisoner.

JOHN: Thou art his keeper.

HUBERT: And I'll keep him so
that he shall not offend your majesty.

JOHN: Death.

HUBERT: My lord?

JOHN: A grave.

HUBERT: He shall not live.

JOHN: Enough.
I could be merry now.

As you prepare to perform

This tiny extract shows clearly the moment of action that lies between cause and effect, even though neither of the speakers directly says what he means.

Think about

1 What is the King ordering, or at least suggesting?

2 What cause has King John to make this suggestion?

3 What do you expect to be the effect of this conversation?

Good playwrights make their cause and effect clear, but they do not always give the audience what they expect. Shakespeare gives us the effect we are expecting — but not at all how we expect it! For example, as the play progresses, Hubert duly arranges to have the prince first blinded, then killed. However, in a long scene of almost unbearable tension, he allows himself to talk to his victim, and then can no longer go through with the dreadful deed. Arthur escapes unscathed, though still a prisoner.

Thank goodness, because King John, too, has had a change of heart. He wants the boy alive and free. But Shakespeare has not finished with us yet. Hubert is told to free the young prisoner. But Arthur does not know that, and believes his life is still in danger. Desperate to gain his freedom, he leaps from the castle walls, and kills himself only moments before Hubert comes to release him.

But, returning to our moment of action, all this lies in the future. Look again at the passage.

1   Why might the King and Hubert say so little?

2   The Royal war tent where this scene is set is full of people. They are all talking about the battle which has just finished, and what the victory means. How might this affect the way Hubert and the King have their conversation?

3   Until this moment, King John has not been a real villain — certainly his lords do not think he is one. How will this affect his timing of his suggestion?

4   Would they be speaking quickly, slowly or a mixture of both? Are there any key pauses?

5   Are they being furtive, or somehow showing they do not want to be interrupted?

6   Where are they physically in relation to each other? Standing? Either of them sitting? Might they use furniture, or hands, to screen their conversation from the others?

Try out the scene

In pairs, play the scene. You should try it a few times, pausing at different points to see how that affects the power of the moment.

6 Language

In drama, as in real life, we express our ideas, our feelings and our needs to each other by:
- the words we say
- the way we say them
- our body language.

Together these make up the language of the drama.

Activity
1

Make groups of five. Three to improvise, and two to monitor. Try the following scene.

Cont.

Roles:	Two parents and their child.
Context:	All have agreed to meet in town to go to a very special show. Parent **A**, who has the tickets, arrives very late, so that the family misses the first half.
Constraints:	It is an ordinary, caring family, and the parents do not want the child to be affected by the argument.
Monitor 1:	Take notes on the language — *the kinds of words used*: <ul><li>Is there any swearing?</li><li>Are words used that the child would not understand?</li><li>Is it ordinary, domestic language, or is it heightened in any way?</li><li>Do all three characters use the same language?</li></ul>
Monitor 2:	Take notes on *the way the characters talk*: <ul><li>The volume — how do they use their voices — shrill or murmuring?</li><li>Is there variety of pitch?</li><li>What about their body language, gestures and signals — how do they stand or sit; what are their eyes and faces doing?</li></ul>

At the end, monitors share with the improvisers what you have observed.

Activity 2

In the same groups, now try this scene.

Roles:	Two priests and a child king or queen. The player who was parent **A** now plays priest **A**, the child is now the king or queen.
Context:	In ancient Egypt, a great ceremony has been prepared, to pray to the gods for rain to flood the Nile and make it fertile. Priest **A**, who is bringing the sacrifice, has arrived late and has ruined the ceremony, maybe offending the gods.
Constraints:	The priests are sincere; they are respected elders. They do not want their young mon-

arch to know what damage may have been caused.

Monitors: Again, observe carefully and take notes on the kinds of language used and the way the characters talk — as you did in the last scene. At the end, share your findings with the players.

Activity 3

Comparing scenes you will have noticed a lot of difference in the language, voice and body language of all three characters.

Look carefully at the monitors' notes of one of the scenes and take note of the particular words, intonations and gestures they picked out. Now try playing the other scene, using that kind of language.

Comic? Silly? Or just frustrating and unbelievable? Of course, because the language is now wrong!

The language of drama

As we saw in Chapter 1, dramatic language is shaped by three factors: the situation, the roles and the relationships. For the drama to work, the language must convey these convincingly and appropriately.

Situation

You wouldn't expect ancient priests to talk about cinema tickets, nor modern parents to address their children with: 'O Child . . .' Even within a particular time or place there are different languages, or registers, for different occasions. This is as true in real life as it is in drama. All of you have the register you use with your friends in the school yard, the one you use in a school assembly for thanking an outside visitor, the one you use with your grandparents, the one you use in church, the one you use in showing a rival gang how tough you are. Each register has its own vocabulary and speaking characteristics, which are inappropriate, and may even be taboo, in other situations.

Roles

The register depends not only on the situation, but also on your role and purpose in the action. You may have noticed in the first improvisation that the parents' registers were similar, but the child's was a bit different. You might explore this a little further.

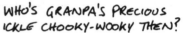

WHO'S GRANPA'S PRECIOUS ICKLE CHOOKY-WOOKY THEN?

Activity 4

Try playing out the first scene again. The situation will remain the same, but we will change the roles slightly.

Improvisers: **A** and **B**, instead of being parents, are modern priests, taking a group of disadvantaged children to a special show. **C** is one of those children.

Monitors: Take notes on how this scene differs from Activity 1 in its verbal and non-verbal language.

At the end, again share your findings with the improvisers. You will probably find both differences and similarities.

Relationships

The language of drama is further modified by what the characters feel for each other, and by their relative status.

Consider character **C** in these improvisations: as a child, he or she is lower in status than the adults, but as a child-monarch, higher. Now consider **A** and **B**. As parents or priests, how would their feelings towards each other affect their language? Try out these two variations:

- **A** and **B** loving or respecting each other
- **A** and **B** hating each other.

You are likely to find some striking differences in their language, both in the kind of words they use, and in their body language.

Language and image

You'll have already noticed language is more than just words. Now let's see how words and movement combine to create dramatic imagery.

Activity
5

1   Divide into groups of four.

2   Each group is to build an improvisation in which each member of the group speaks three blocks of language. A block of language is quite substantial — perhaps a couple of sentences. For example:

'Hello, Tom. Have you managed to fix the brakes yet? I've got to pick up Mum at 5.30.'

'So, you dare to enter into the palace of your king. Speak now, before you are silenced forever.'

Notice how in these examples the situation, roles and relationships are indicated clearly.

3   You can speak in any order you like, each developing the situation as it grows. Just be sure that you only use three blocks of language each; no more, no less.

4   When all groups have prepared their work and feel comfortable with it, present it to the other members of the class.

Activity 6

1 In the same groups, re-work your improvisations replacing each block of language with *three words only*. This means that each participant speaks nine words (three groups of three words).

2 You must keep the original meaning of your first improvisation, so give careful thought to the way you can express meaning through body language and the way you speak.

3 Present this second version to your classmates. Did you feel it worked more effectively? Which 'blocks' were improved? Which suffered?

Activity 7

1 Now re-work the improvisation one last time, replacing each group of three words with *one word only*. Each participant will now speak three words in total. Each word will now do the job of a whole block of language.

2 You will have to work even harder now to devise ways of conveying your original meaning.

3 Present this third version to the class. Did you feel it worked effectively? What was improved? What was made unclear?

Economy

Language works best when it is used with economy. It is easy for participants to 'overtalk' in improvisation, using vague statements and repetition which don't advance or clarify the action. You should never talk for the sake of 'doing something'; what you say should always add to, or be in agreement with, the context, your role, and the way the action is developing.

No doubt, there were several occasions during the previous activities when you felt that fewer words worked better than the long block of language. This economy of language proved successful because it was strengthened by non-verbal images.

Images

Dramatic action is made up of language and movement. Our movement creates visual images which help convey meaning. When the language available to you was restricted, you had to rely much more on visual images to make your meaning clear. Dramatic action is enriched when physical images are carefully used to reinforce and strengthen the language. List occasions when this happened in the improvisation you developed.

Images and language can also be managed in such a way that they contradict each other. Imagine, for example, the tired mother sitting with her feet up, sipping a coffee and saying, 'Oh, I'm a ball of energy. I've done nothing all day.' Here the physical image is sending a very different message from the verbal language. Have you observed any such contradictions in the activities in this chapter?

In the following activity, you will see both the power of economical language, and how language and image can contradict each other.

Activity 8

Here is yet another variant of the dramatic problem of persons who turn up late, letting down their partners and others who depend on them. The scene, which we have updated to a modern context, is from Shakespeare's *Anthony and Cleopatra*.

Roles: Anthony and Octavius, the joint military dictators of Rome; some reporters and government officials.

Cont.

Background: The dictators are threatened by a rebel uprising. Anthony, the senior, more popular and respected of the two, goes to America to get military aid. There, he becomes completely sidetracked, and spends his time in Hollywood, besotted by the film star, Cleopatra. Magazine photos of them in Californian night clubs get back to Rome. Imagine how Octavius feels!

Context: Anthony returns, without the military aid. How does he feel, stepping off the plane, knowing he has let Octavius down, but also knowing he has to save face.

Setting: The airport lounge. Octavius, other government officials and reporters are officially welcoming Anthony home. There are two seats ready for a television interview.

Constraints: Anthony and Octavius will have plenty to say to each other, but the TV cameras and their colleagues are all around, so they must maintain a united front.

Management: 1 In pairs, try the scene first with your own words. Start with Anthony at least five metres away, walking towards the welcoming party.

2 Now, here are Shakespeare's words, which we have deliberately left unpunctuated:

OCTAVIUS: Welcome to Rome
ANTHONY: Thank you
OCTAVIUS: Sit
ANTHONY: Sit sir
OCTAVIUS: Nay then
[which can mean either 'all right' or 'no'!]

3 Learn the words (it shouldn't be too hard!).

4 You can say the words in quite different ways with different results. Why does Anthony, the senior partner, use the word 'Sir'? Should there be a full stop after it, or a question mark, or three dots . . .? Who sits down? Anthony or Octavius, both or neither? Are there long pauses?

5 After you have tried out the scene a

couple of times, form groups of seven or eight. This scene is very public, with friends of each speaker, reporters and others. Do they have an effect on the power game? Are Anthony and Octavius aware of them?

6 Now try the scene again. Remember to start with that five metre walk.

The text from *Anthony and Cleopatra* is very ambiguous. You will probably find that different groups in the class end up with totally different seating arrangements, according to whether Octavius or Anthony gets the upper hand, or a stalemate results. There are no right answers in the words themselves. You would need to read the whole play to decide finally. However, it is wonderfully rich in possibilities.

Do you notice also how economical it is? Five pieces of conversation, which express a very complex relationship and a very tense moment, all in ten words, within a single line of Shakespeare's blank verse.

And in plays . . .

Extract 8: from *The Fourth Year are Animals*

This scene is part of a drama lesson. In the play it takes place before the scene in the museum, and it, too, is about ancient Egypt. Alan is valiantly trying to create some atmosphere, and Kelly, for a change, is behaving herself.

ALAN: Now I want us to imagine that Arthur is the Pharaoh — the Great King over all of us. And our Pharaoh has died.

(ARTHUR *closes his eyes but remains sitting upright.*)

So what we must do now is to bring our precious objects and give them to be buried with our Pharaoh. So one by one can we do that?

(KELLY *comes first. She gently places her imaginary object in* ARTHUR'S *hand and kneels to place her forehead on* ARTHUR'S *knee. Then, quietly . . .*)

KELLY: He should be lying down, Sir, if he's dead.

ALAN: All right — lie down Arthur.

(*Gently they lay* ARTHUR *out on the podium.*)

KELLY: Just a minute, Sir.

(*She runs from the room and exits.*)

ALAN: Kelly, where are you going?

(*She is gone, so he returns to the rest of the class.*)

Now think about our Pharaoh. Think about what he meant to us when he was alive. He was our King who looked after his people . . .

(KELLY *returns with a roll of toilet paper, with which she begins to wrap* ARTHUR *up.*)

KELLY: Like in the Mummy's Tomb, Sir.

(ALAN *has no option but to go along with her idea.*)

ALAN: As we are wrapping our King we do it with respect for him, with honour and love . . .

(*The public address speaker crackles into life and a voice announces . . .*)

VOICE: Could I have your attention please? The ladies in the canteen would like to advise us that as of next Tuesday the price of pasties will be thirty-seven pence instead of thirty-five. Thank you.

(*Any atmosphere which had built up has now been destroyed.*)

ARTHUR: Not on me mouth.

KELLY: We have to Arthur — your majesty.

ALAN: We must be gentle with our King, with the body of our Pharaoh.

(*Again the speaker crackles.*)

VOICE: Those students who will be going swimming this afternoon are to meet Mr Keaven by the Brandon St. gate at 1.45. That's all; Mr Keaven's swimming group to the Brandon St. gate at 1.45. Thank you.

ALAN: (*Valiantly carrying on*) Our King has saved us from floods and fires, from locust plagues and famine . . .

ARTHUR: It's too tight.

KELLY: (*Hitting him*) Shut up Arthur — you're dead.

As you prepare to perform

Think about

At least four quite different registers (see page 77) are being used here.

1   *Alan*: he is using an almost biblical style.
   - Why does he do this?
   - Which words and sentence structures can you identify which give this biblical flavour?

2   *Arthur*: this is all far too hard for poor Arthur, who doesn't really know why he's being asked to lie down and be wrapped in toilet paper anyway.
   - What do you notice about the only two things he manages to say?

3   *Kelly*: she is trying hard to be involved, but her language is still almost entirely in her natural school-room register.
   - Just once she gets it right. When?
   - Which of her words and phrases most destroys the atmosphere of 'The Land of The Pharaohs'?
   - There is nothing wrong with her bright idea of wrapping up the Mummy. However, what effect does her use of the toilet paper have on the drama?

4   *The PA system*: when the public address speaker 'crackles into life', it does so in language that neither Alan nor the students would use. 'As of next Tuesday' is a clumsy and pompous phrase; pasties and swimming groups hardly belong in the land of the Pharaohs either. If you have been in a school where there is a PA system, you will know how loud, distorted and tinny they can sound.
   - Can you find other phrases that are particularly jarring?
   - What effect does the PA system have on the lesson?

Try out the scene

All these registers clash, and that is part of the painful comedy of the scene. As you act it out, if possible with a bad microphone and speaker for the PA system, make the most of these clashes. The physical action and images back up the clashes, too, so you should have fun with the toilet paper, and Arthur's helpless incomprehension.

Voice

The words we speak and the images which accompany them create meaning, for ourselves as participants in improvisations, and for audiences watching a play or film. However, there is a third factor which helps create dramatic meaning: *the way the words are said.* The delivery of language tells a great deal about the speaker's intentions and opinions. Often the way something is spoken says more than the words themselves.

In pairs, improvise this scene.

Roles: A parent and a 17-year-old daughter or son.

Context: The parent is reading the paper. The teenager wants to borrow the family car (you decide why).

Constraints: 1 The parent may only use the word 'No' in response to the repeated requests for the car.

2 The parent, who won't be needing the car, is uncertain about refusing. If your child convinces you, then maybe you'll say 'Yes'. It's up to you.

3 Remember, parents can only ever reply with 'No' — except maybe one final 'Yes'.

In the same pairs, play the scene again. This time, the parent won't let the 17-year-old have the car — it's impossible (you decide why).

The parent must answer 'No' to every request — even the final one.

It's how you say it

Was that last scene hard to play out? The teenager should have realised very swiftly that the whole thing was a waste of time. In the first exercise, the parent's uncertainty would have been clear and it would have always seemed possible that the child might end up with the car. Did you receive it in the end?

On each occasion, although the parent could only say 'No', quite different meanings were being created, perhaps leading to quite different outcomes. The way the parent said 'No' was what mattered.

Activity 11

Roles:	Make pairs, **A** and **B**. The relationship will emerge in the improvisation.
Setting:	At the breakfast table.
Context:	**A** and **B** begin in a friendly way, then one says something to anger the other. A row develops, and becomes quite heated. Finally, one apologises, the argument ends, and they are friends again.
Constraints:	In this improvision you cannot speak in English. Instead you must talk in a made-up foreign language. Of course, it will just be garbled sound, but you will be able to capture the rhythms and pattern of human speech.

Aspects of voice

In Activity 11 you were not using language, just the voice and strange sounds to create your meaning. Even though you couldn't understand the words, the pattern of argument, apology and friendship is quite clear. Even subtle variations in voice can convey quite different meanings.

The following list introduces some technical terms which will enable you to understand and describe the way voice and speech are managed in drama. Being able to describe the way the voice is used will help you to increase your flexibility and control over it when using text and in improvisations.

1 Sound and silence: listen for the silences which occur. When are the pauses longest? Shortest?

2 Pitch: listen for variation in the height or depth of the sound. As an argument builds do the voices become higher?

3 Pace: listen for variation in the speed of delivery. When is the sound coming thick and fast? Slow and deliberate?

4 Intonation: note changes in the rise or fall of the sound at the end of sentences. What happens when questions are asked? Demands are made?

5 Volume: listen for changes in loudness or softness. When is the voice most loud? Most soft?

6 Tone colour: note differences in the quality of the voice. Is it warm and understanding? Cold and abrupt? Aggressive and hot?

7 Emphasis: listen for the sounds which are stressed. How are certain sounds emphasised? When do stresses increase?

Activity 12

Select one or two pairs to act out the improvisation they devised in Activity 11. As they do so, note the variations in voice as listed above.

Discuss your findings with others in the class. Your discussions may be helped if you tape record the improvised argument, and then play it back for clarification.

Activity 13

Our final activity — and we use real words at last! This exercise requires you to manipulate and play with the following text.

A: You're late.
B: I'm sorry.
A: Well — did you find anything?
B: In a way.
A: What do you mean?
B: But not what you expected.
A: Go on.
B: It was very dark. I couldn't see. This is what I found.
A: It looks like you were right then.

1   Form pairs, **A** and **B**.

2   Learn the lines allocated to you.

3   With your partner, discuss the possible contexts, subtexts and relationships in the text.

4 Select two quite different interpretations of the text and practise them, making sure the meaning is clear in each case.

5 Tape record each of your interpretations.

6 Swap your tape recordings with another pair of students and listen carefully to the interpretations on tape, a number of times if necessary. Compare the interpretations.
- What meaning is created by each interpretation?
- How is voice used to make that meaning clear?

Consider specific variations in the use of silence, pitch, pace, volume, intonation, emphasis and tone colour.

7 Share your findings with the pair who recorded the interpretation.

7 Movement

Drama has traditionally been stored in books, or playscripts, which consist of words. Working through this book, you will be aware that drama is really action. Words are only a small part of that action. Film and video are modern ways of storing drama which store images as well as words. In fact, the images are usually much more important than the words. You can watch a thriller movie with the sound turned down, or in a foreign language, and still follow what is going on. However, the images which film and video store are only two-dimensional. In the theatre and in improvised drama the action is in real space; with real breathing, sweating bodies expressing real feelings, holding and moving real things.

Images in action: the Death in the Village drama

Movement, like language, is dictated by situation, roles and relationships. This is obvious if you consider that Zola Budd and Mary Decker might race together, but they are hardly likely to dance together. Of course, the opportunities are plenty for absurd comedy, if you link movement with situations that don't fit: The Battle of Waterloo played as a ballet, or the conquest of Everest by people in wheelchairs!

In this chapter we are going to show how situation, roles and relationships open up possibilities for movement which will enrich the action, and create more powerful meaning.

Look at the painting by Mary Joseph inside the back cover. From the earliest British settlement in Australia, there was a determined aboriginal resistance to the white invasion. All too often the outcome of these unequal confrontations was heavy aboriginal casualties. This painting is of one such violent clash known as the 'Coniston Massacre' which occurred as recently as 1928. After four years of drought in the desert outback, the aborigines were forced to compete with the settler's sheep and cattle for the limited water resources.

The flashpoint came when the aborigines killed a white dingo trapper. A party of white settlers, led by Mounted Constable William Murray, attacked the aboriginal tribe where they were engaged in their ceremonies. Officially 31 blacks were killed, although tribal accounts put the number as high as 100 men, women and children. Still today the Walbiri people remember these events as 'the killing times'.

Do you see any similarities with Goya's painting, *The Third of May*? The style is different, the landscape and characters very much so, but isn't the story much the same? An execution or massacre of unarmed civilians, by foreigners, in reprisal for some killings of their people. As with the Goya, our sympathy is with the victims, so helpless in the face of the still figure holding the gun. And there is another similarity: both painters are of the victims' own culture. A French person could not have painted the Goya, nor a white have painted Mary Joseph's with so much feeling.

You may feel that you have explored executions far enough after Chapter 5. Never mind, the story may be similar, but our approach will be quite different. We do not need to explore roles and relationships again — what it feels like to be a member of a firing squad or a victim. We did that in our Goya drama, and you can use what you discovered there. Here, we will be using movement to help explore and interpret the very different imagery and mood of this picture, and what it means.

Movement and stillness

In the frozen moment of this painting, there is much movement suggested. The word 'moment' originally comes from the word 'movement'. Where there are people, our eye always expects to see movement — stare closely at the picture, and you may find the figures seem to move as your eye travels. When people are 'frozen', the moment is made significant because it is unexpected.

Activity 1

Musical statues

We will start, unexpectedly, to explore the execution in Mary Joseph's painting by playing a party game.

1 The class decides together on a frozen group scene — on a beach, perhaps at a night club or a street accident. One person will be the Controller.

Cont.

2 Get into position as characters in that scene, doing something relevant and interesting that involves continuous movement (not just sun-bathing!).

3 The Controller starts playing some music, during which the figures must move continuously. Whenever the Controller stops the music, everybody must stop, instantly, and freeze in whatever position they find themselves, or they are out of the game.

As you play, you will note that some of the frozen positions look quite odd, or even absurd. When moving, they looked quite sensible.

Activity 2

Life in the village

Play the game again. This time, the scene is one of village life (not necessarily Aboriginal). People are going about their everyday tasks, which again involve continuous movement. But the atmosphere has changed: danger is in the air. The Controller substitutes a drum or tambour for the music, and sets up a slow, menacing beat. The freeze signal is a loud, single beat, then silence. When everybody freezes, it is in order to listen, intently, for the approach of the enemy.

Activity 3

Fate is a gun

Appoint a second Controller, *Fate*, who holds a pointer representing a gun. The village is surrounded by a reprisal party. Your drama space is the compound that you are trapped inside. The first Controller drums as before, but sometimes fast, sometimes slow. The villagers move to the speed of the drumbeat, trying to avoid the pointer, which Fate moves slowly, randomly, around. (It is probably more effective if you don't hold it as a gun, but more as the 'Pointer of Fate'.) When the freeze beat happens, the figure of Fate alone can move, to touch with the pointer that villager closest in line with it. That villager must immediately fall to the floor, exactly where he or she is, and take no further part. When the movement begins again, the others must be careful to avoid those figures.

As the game progresses, note the contrast between the villagers' first fleeing, then frozen terror, and the slow stalking of Fate. Now there is a new quality creeping in, the contrast between the fleeing figures and the motionless corpses.

From game to drama

As a kind of drama through movement, games should not be underestimated. They may be fun, but they are certainly not silly. You may know that 'ring a' roses' re-enacts the great plague of London, 'red rover' is a war-game . . . and we have just made 'musical statues' symbolic of an aboriginal mass-acre.

It may be that the games you just played merely stayed good fun, like a version of tag. Maybe though, some of the power of what the game was representing did seep into the work, if you were conscious of Mary Joseph's painting, and maintained a serious, tense atmosphere. If so, the contrast between movement and stillness would have contributed to that effect.

Contrast

Look again at the painting. See how the painter uses colour to pick out and emphasise the stillness among all that movement. All the running figures are black, but the trees and the mountains are solid blocks of colour. The rearing horse is black, but see how sinister the mounted white man is, so precisely painted and still. His very colourfulness is wrong, out of place. Note too the defiant brown slash of the boomerang thrower, and the pitiful red splashes anchoring the fallen victims.

In the next exercise, as you explore contrasts in movement, think about ways you can manage your space. Explore the patterns you create — symmetrical and asymmetrical. Explore variations in:
- rhythm and pace
- physical levels and directions
- proxemics (your distance and position relative to others).

As you discover the best way to manage your movement the game will become more dramatic.

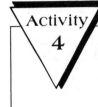

Activity 4

We all fall down

Go back to the game as you played it last and re-enact it. Don't try to make it look literally like the painting. It's still a game, remember. However, as you play, explore that contrast between movement and stillness. Use the drumbeat consciously to control it, and experiment with managing the space.

Expressive movement

Returning to the painting, we can start to see how movement expresses not only the action (what's happening), but the mood and symbols — what it all means. The story of the painting is becoming expressive dance, in fact. Don't worry if you don't feel you can dance properly. Neither can we, and it doesn't matter.

Activity 5

The life of our people

Eventually this activity will involve the whole class, but for sections of it you will need to work by yourself or with small groups.

1 Go back to Activity 2 and play it again. Look very carefully at the sequence of movements which you were doing: the actions and skills of being a villager.

2 Take a sequence of about one minute from Activity 2, and re-enact exactly what you did. It does not matter whether or not it was an aboriginal village you chose; we are not trying to reproduce the painting. It is your village now. If your activity involves working with other members of the class, so much the better.

3 What you did in Activity 2 was probably sketchy. Take the time now to fill in the details. Give the village a sensible name, and agree upon:
  • what sort of a village it is
  • what climate it has
  • what skills you might need to survive.

4 Now answer: If I really were one of those villagers, what precisely would I be doing? This is important; getting your sequence of movements right actually helps in developing belief and understanding in your character, even when you are only doing it in mime.

5 Now use the Controller with the drum. Take a fairly brisk beat, and re-enact the movement sequence. Try to find some kind of rhythm to the movements, even if it makes them less realistic.

6 Now take a section, not more than half of the sequence, which involved the most interesting or significant movements. Go through it again, but make it twice as big as real life (that is, exaggerate the movements), and slow it down to half pace. (Yes, it may look a bit silly at this stage.)

7 Keeping it to half pace, try it to the original brisk drumbeat. When you have finished, find a way of starting again without breaking off, so it becomes a continuous sequence, like a film or tape loop. Experiment with it a bit, and fit it in with other people's sequences.

8 Eventually you will have a movement event in one or more groups, which represents the activities of your village. You have just created *The dance of the life of our people.*

Activity 6

The emblem

Take a rest now! Find some art materials, and, from what you have discovered about your village, create with care its emblem. An emblem is a visible object symbolizing the community. It may be a single statue or monument, a sacred picture or icon, or a carving. Alternatively, it may be a badge, necklace or apron which you all wear.

Now, in some way, incorporate that emblem in your dance. Create a ritual or ceremony to make it important. If it is a statue, it might become the focus of the dance itself. If it is a necklace or badge, putting it on will be a special moment.

Activity 7

The death of our people

1 Now go back to Activity 3. Re-create the movements you used when trying to escape and being cut down one by one.

Cont.

2 Build this into a whole-group dance sequence in the same way as you did for Activity 5, step by step. Remember this time to bring out the power of stillness among movement. Look again at Mary Joseph's painting to see the patterns of movement, running away and lying still that she uses.

3 Perhaps you could build the sequence around the figure of Fate holding the pointer. Use an appropriately varied drumbeat.

4 Finally, make the climax of your dance the symbolic destruction of the village emblem — perhaps deliberately or carelessly by the executioners, or perhaps by the dying villagers themselves. Do not actually destroy your emblem yet.

5 Now you have created *The dance of the death of our people*. Put the two dances together to make one: *The dance of our history*. Now you have a symbolic re-telling of the drama that lies behind Mary Joseph's painting.

Activity 8

Laying the ghosts

We are now ready to bring out all the power of Mary Joseph's dramatic moment. To do this we will put the dance into a truly dramatic frame, outside the event.

Date: Generations later, the anniversary of the massacre.

Roles: The descendants of the survivors of the massacre; a foreign visitor.

Context: Every year the villagers gather secretly to dance their history, to keep alive the memory. This year a foreigner is living with the villagers, maybe as a doctor or a researcher into the tribe's customs.

Constraints: **1** The descendants have neither forgotten nor forgiven the foreign executioners.

2 The villagers like the foreigner so they tolerate the intrusion. The stranger is friendly and sympathetic, but is, nevertheless, a representative of the executioners' culture.

Management: This year the dance has an added dimension. The villagers are offering the stranger the chance to be initiated as one of them. By this act, the stranger can wipe out the foreigners' blood-guilt. However, in order to do this, the stranger will have to acknowledge that guilt, and repudiate his or her own people.

At the end of the dance, after the emblem has been destroyed, the stranger will have to make a choice:
- step into the dance, take the pointer of Fate, and break it
- sit still, aloof and apart.

The choice will be seen in the movement or the stillness.

Outcome: Will the ghosts of the past be laid to rest? Will the dance be so eloquent and powerful that the stranger will be convinced to repudiate his or her people and break the gun?

This painting and drama were drawn from real life events — shocking events, but ones which existed in fact and time (from the 6th–27th August 1928). What follows is part of the Australian Government's Board of Enquiry (January 1929) into the Coniston Massacre.

CHAIRMAN: You made a report dated 2 September 1928, but you did not mention that a fifth aboriginal woman had been badly wounded. Apparently she died but you did not seem to think it important to detail when this happened?

CONSTABLE MURRAY: I don't think it matters whether she died a minute or hour afterwards.

CHAIRMAN: You refer to your tracker shooting a fleeing native with a rifle. You didn't report that either.

CONSTABLE MURRAY: I mentioned the fact that natives were killed but I did not think it necessary to say who killed them.

CHAIRMAN: If these blacks had been whites would your attitude have been any different?

CONSTABLE MURRAY: I would not have considered it necessary to say more than that they had been killed by the party.

CHAIRMAN: Did you in your report give the number killed?

CONSTABLE MURRAY: No.

CHAIRMAN: Why?

CONSTABLE MURRAY: I did not think it necessary at the time.

CHAIRMAN: If you were giving a report about the killing of the white people would you think it necessary?

CONSTABLE MURRAY: Yes.

CHAIRMAN: What police experience did you have before joining the Central Australia Police?

CONSTABLE MURRAY: None.

CHAIRMAN: Have you ever undergone any course of instruction in police duties?

CONSTABLE MURRAY: No.

The Board's findings were:

The evidence of all witnesses was inconclusive, and, after exhaustive enquiry lasting three weeks, the Board found the shooting was justified, and that the natives killed in the various encounters ... were on a marauding expedition, with the avowed object of wiping out the white settlers, and the native boys on these stations.

a. In respect to the shooting of 17 natives ... the shooting was justified.
b. Respecting the shooting of 14 natives ... the shooting was justified.

Although your drama was not directly about Coniston, it was inspired by the painting, so you probably have a strong reaction to these findings. Has reading this put the drama in a new light for you? Does the drama which you have done put this verdict in a new light? If so, it may be because the transcript — and the whole Enquiry — seems so cool and unlike your drama. You *lived through* the events. The transcript was just *reporting* them, so it had to be free of passion and emotions — in a *dispassionate* register.

Activity 9

Imagine that some years later, the Stranger in the final scene of your drama is in Britain being interviewed on his/her experience with the Villagers. Can you write the transcript of that interview, led by a dispassionate interviewer?

By that cold and distant style, the Board of Enquiry into the Coniston Massacre gives the impression that their findings are fair and unbiased. Do you think they were? (Some people even at the time described the report as a 'whitewash'.)

Activity 10

Look again at Mary Joseph's painting, study carefully the Coniston transcript and recall the way you felt as a Villager in the *Death in the Village* drama. Now, if you were the Chairperson of that Board of Enquiry, what would be your verdict?

Adopting the same dispassionate style as the original, hand down your full report. Deliver it live or taped, or publish it formally in writing.

And in plays . . .

Extract 9: From *The Insect Play* by Josef and Karel Capek

This classic, funny and chilling fable was first produced in 1923, just after World War 1. Now, as you will see from this short extract, it seems to be prophetic (Josef Capek died in a Nazi concentration camp; his brother Karel died just after Hitler's invasion of their beloved Czechoslovakia).

The playwrights examine human society by comparing it to the insect world. Apart from an old drunken tramp, who is a kind of human observer, all the characters are insects, so the opportunities for movement are rich. In Act 1, the tramp meets the traditional upper classes, the butterflies, beautiful, callous and self-centred. In Act 2 he looks at the capitalistic middle classes, bugs and beetles, ruthlessly devouring each other as they pursue profit and personal security.

Our extract is taken from Act 3, where the tramp is still searching for what makes humans greater than insects. He stumbles over an ant-heap, a totalitarian dictatorship where individual struggles are submerged in the 'common good'.

BLIND ANT: (*More quickly*) Blank, two, three, four — blank, two —

CHIEF ENGINEER: We must quicken the speed.

2ND ENGINEER: The speed of output.

CHIEF ENGINEER: The Peace of Life —

2ND ENGINEER: Every movement must be quickened.

CHIEF ENGINEER: Shortened —

2ND ENGINEER: Calculated —

CHIEF ENGINEER: To a second —

2ND ENGINEER: To the nth of a second —

CHIEF ENGINEER: So as to save time —

2ND ENGINEER: So as to increase the output —

CHIEF ENGINEER: Work has been too slow — labour must be carried out unsparingly —

2ND ENGINEER: Ruthlessly —

TRAMP: And what's the hurry, anyway?

CHIEF ENGINEER: The interests of the whole.

2ND ENGINEER: It is a question of output — question of power.

CHIEF ENGINEER: Peaceful competition.

2ND ENGINEER: We are fighting the battle of peace.

· · ·

CHIEF ENGINEER: Faster — faster —

(An ANT *collapses with its load and moans*)

2ND ENGINEER: Tut, tut! What's that? Get up!

ANOTHER ANT: Dead!

CHIEF ENGINEER: One, two — carry him away, quick.

2ND ENGINEER: He died honourably in the cause of speed.

CHIEF ENGINEER: How are you lifting him? Too slowly, you're wasting time. Drop him. Now head and feet together. Blank, two, three — wrong, drop him again. Head and feet — blank, two, three, four — take him away — blank, two, blank, two, blank —

2ND ENGINEER: Two, three, four — quicker.

TRAMP: Anyhow, he died quick enough —

CHIEF ENGINEER: Work, work, he who possesses more, must work more.

2ND ENGINEER: He requires more —

CHIEF ENGINEER: He has more to defend —

2ND ENGINEER: And more to gain.

CHIEF ENGINEER: We are a nation of peace — peace means work.

2ND ENGINEER: And work, strength.

CHIEF ENGINEER: And strength, war.

2ND ENGINEER: Yes, yes!

As you prepare to perform

It may not seem as if there is very much movement at first reading, but while the engineers are talking, the stage is actually teeming with ants, all working to the beat of the blind ant's counting.

If you have access to this play, look at some of the other acts, the creepers and crawlers especially, and see how insect movement possibilities enrich the action.

Think about

1   What might their movements be? Remember, they are ants. Their leaders are called engineers — that should give you another movement clue.

2   What kinds of tasks might they be doing, for what reasons?

3   When the ant collapses, what happens to the drumbeat and the movements?

Try out the scene

1   Improvise whatever sort of movement seems appropriate to you.

2   When you have decided on basic movements, spread them so that they take up the whole space — in clumps, lines, circles, with varied movement patterns, contrasting and interesting. Can you use different height levels? What about varying the size of the movements, making them minute or exaggerated? Symmetry and balance will be very important to help give the sense of automatons.

3   Experiment with giving the ants burdens; sticks, rods or ropes to link them.

4   Now fit the movements to the beat of the blind ant who has a drum.

5   When the ant collapses, experiment with them all getting out of control and chaotic, until the Chief pulls them back into order.

8   Mood

Remember when you arrived for your first day of secondary school — how did you feel? Or when your school was given an unexpected holiday — how did you feel then?

Your feelings about each of these events would have been different but there would have been strong emotions associated with them. Everybody starting secondary school feels apprehensive and uncertain, while most are thrilled at an unexpected holiday. There is a shared mood and atmosphere created by the event.

Creating mood

Put together all the elements we have investigated so far and we have mood. It is the feeling or atmosphere that is created by, and emerges through, the dramatic action. In this chapter, we look at ways mood can be built into the drama.

Activity 1

Roles:	Make pairs: **A** is a student of about your age; **B** is one of **A**'s parents.
Context:	**A** has arrived home from school and gone straight to his or her bedroom, obviously upset about something. The parent waits a while, then knocks and enters. The parent tries to find out what the problem is.

Constraints:	At school **A** was embarrassed and hurt in front of friends (you decide why — perhaps a harsh comment from an unthinking teacher, perhaps teasing by insensitive students). **A** is hurt and doesn't really want to talk about it.
	    The parent is to be sympathetic and supportive, and must find out what the problem is as gently as possible.
	    Let the role-play build slowly.

Outcome:	Let the outcome emerge from the action. Is the problem revealed?

Well, did you find out? Before we discuss the mood created in this role-play, try one more.

Activity 2

Roles:	Make groups of four. **A**, **B**, **C** and **D** are all members of a high-powered, successful computer firm. **A** is the boss, overworked and fast talking. **B** is personal assistant to the boss, extremely efficient and fast talking. **C** is a top salesperson, successful and fast talking. **D** is personal secretary to the top salesperson, fussy and fast talking.
Context:	**1** Sales have slumped and **C** is trying to convince the boss to spend an extra $100 000 on television advertising. The decision must be made urgently. **2** **B** and **D** must keep interrupting the discussion between **A** and **C** (perhaps a letter to be signed, perhaps an urgent telephone call — make the reasons up).

Cont.

3 **A** and **C** must deal quickly with these interruptions before returning to their discussion.

4 Let the action develop with constant interruption and speedy problem solving.

Outcome: After about three minutes **B** advises that **A** is running late for an important appointment, and must leave at once. **A** hurries off, making a decision before leaving.

Establishing mood

Each of these role-plays established a particular mood, but a quite different one in each case. The first had a quality of intimacy and sensitive inquiry; the second of frantic, chaotic decision making. What factors created these two different moods?

Activity
3

With a partner discuss how each of the elements of drama were used in the two role-plays. List the differences as you isolate them.

Element of Drama	Activity 1 *'What happened at school today'*	Activity 2 *'The advertising 'campaign'*
Tension		
Focus		
Time		
Place		
Language		
Movement		

Mood and tension

From the lists you just created, it is clear the elements of drama were used in different ways. Because of this, different moods were created. No doubt you will have already noticed that mood is something we feel about the dramatic action. In this way it is closely linked with tension; as the tension in a drama builds so too does the mood. Then, as the mood builds, it in turn strengthens the tension. But the mood of a piece of dramatic action can change too, often in response to a change in the source of tension.

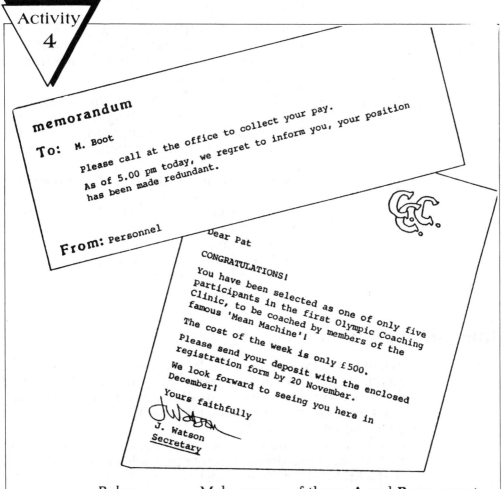

Activity 4

memorandum

To: M. Boot

Please call at the office to collect your pay. As of 5.00 pm today, we regret to inform you, your position has been made redundant.

From: Personnel

Dear Pat

CONGRATULATIONS!

You have been selected as one of only five participants in the first Olympic Coaching Clinic, to be coached by members of the famous 'Mean Machine'!

The cost of the week is only £500. Please send your deposit with the enclosed registration form by 20 November. We look forward to seeing you here in December!

Yours faithfully

J. Watson
Secretary

Roles: Make groups of three. **A** and **B** are parents of **C**, who is a promising swimmer, one of the best in the country. **C** loves swimming and **A** and **B** are proud of their child.

Cont.

Context: A arrives home from work with bad news for **B**: **A** has been sacked and is out of work. The chief cause of concern is how the family will manage financially on a greatly reduced income. At the appropriate moment, **C** arrives home from school full of news and excitement, having been selected to attend a special swimming coaching clinic in California. It will cost £500 for the week.

Management: Let the improvisation develop slowly, taking the time necessary for the first mood to develop, before introducing **C**.

Outcome: You decide the outcome. Will the money be found for the coaching clinic? Don't jump to an easy, unreal solution (eg suddenly finding you've won the pools).

Discuss: Well, did you give this activity a happy ending or a sad one? As long as it worked for you, either could be appropriate. Spend some time discussing the following questions.
- Did you notice the use of contrasting moods in the activity?
- How would you describe the two contrasting moods? Which was dominant at the end?
- How closely related was the change of mood with the change of tension?

Intensifying mood

In a play or film, the director often uses music to enhance the mood, by appealing to our sense of hearing. In improvised drama we are able to appeal to all five senses to create mood: what we hear, see, and touch (or what touches us); what we taste and what we smell.

A group of 15-year-olds exploring the issue of terrorism in their drama class decided to role-play a hostage situation set in the Middle East. To establish the mood, they devised ways of appealing to each of the five senses. The students divided into two groups — terrorists (five students) and hostages (twenty students). Together they devised the following treatment for the hostages:
- all were blindfolded

- they were made to sit cross-legged on the floor
- their wrists were locked together, as if tied
- middle-eastern music was played
- a stick of incense was burnt
- with their wrists together they were given stale bread to eat
- the terrorists marched up and down, noisily and continuously
- if the hostages moved or acted without instruction they were poked with sticks.

This treatment continued for about twenty minutes. All students (including the hostages) devised these activities with the deliberate intention of creating an appropriate mood. Look back at the activities they set up and see how each affects a different sense. If you like the idea, perhaps you could follow their suggestions and recreate the event for your drama class.

Activity 5

Plan carefully, in groups of five or six, how you will create a mood appropriate for a drama involving a hospital or a shopping centre. What activities will you devise? Will you appeal to all the senses? Set up the activities.

How effective were they? Could any of them be improved?

You could use this mood in a piece of your own dramatic action — exploring life, death, care or negligence in a hospital, or consumer matters, profiteering or busking in a shopping centre.

And in plays . . .

Extract 10: from *Julius Caesar*
by William Shakespeare

This extract is taken from late in the play. Brutus, a Roman general, is preparing for the great battle that will decide his future. A sincere nobleman, he reluctantly joined a plot to kill his over-ambitious friend Julius Caesar. Now he is pursued by an army seeking revenge, led by Mark Anthony. Apprehensively awaiting the battle, Brutus in his tent prepares for bed, with the help of Lucius, his servant. (Lucius agrees to play his lyre to help Brutus sleep. But it is Lucius who falls asleep. Brutus reads on by candlelight, when the light flickers . . .)

BRUTUS: Look, Lucius, here's the book I sought for so;
I put it in the pocket of my gown.

LUCIUS: I was sure your Lordship did not give it me.

BRUTUS: Bear with me, good boy, I am much forgetful.
Cans't thou hold up thy heavy eyes awhile,
And touch thy instrument a strain or two?

LUCIUS: Ay, my lord, an't please you.

BRUTUS: It does, my boy.
I trouble thee too much, but thou art willing.

LUCIUS: It is my duty, sir.

BRUTUS: I should not urge thy duty past thy might;
I know young bloods look for a time of rest.

LUCIUS: I have slept, my lord, already.

BRUTUS: It was well done, and thou shalt sleep again;
I will not hold thee long. If I do live,
I will be good to thee.   (Music, and a song)
This is a sleepy tune: O murd'rous slumber!
Layest thou thy leaden mace upon my boy,
That plays thee music? Gentle knave, good night;
I will not do thee so much wrong to wake thee.
If thou dost nod, thou break'st thy instrument;
I'll take it from thee; and, good boy, good night.
Let me see, let me see; is not the leaf turn'd down
Where I left reading? Here it is, I think.

Enter the Ghost of CAESAR

How ill this taper burns! Ha! who comes here?

I think it is the weakness of mine eyes
That shapes this monstrous apparition.
It comes upon me. Art thou any thing?
Art thou some god, some angel, or some devil,
That mak'st my blood cold, and my hair to stare?
Speak to me what thou art.

GHOST: Thy evil spirit, Brutus.

As you prepare to perform

Did that read easily for you? Shakespeare's text often seems more difficult than it is; it's meant to be performed, not read silently. So, in groups of three, read the text aloud two or three times and then discuss it to clarify any difficult words or phrases. If the meaning is still unclear, discuss it with your teacher or pay a visit to your school's library.

Think about

How will you create the mood of the extract? With your partners list as many words as possible to describe the mood, then consider the following focusing questions.

1 How fast will the scene need to be acted out? Will there be long pauses? Where?

2 How long will Lucius play before he falls asleep? What is Brutus doing while Lucius plays? (He isn't reading — how do we know?)

3 How long does Brutus read before something distracts him?

4 What stage business must be carried out? (The text tells you.) How fast or slow should these actions be completed?

5 How frightened is Brutus by the sight of Caesar's ghost? Does Brutus move across the space after he sees the ghost?

6 How loudly will Brutus and Lucius be talking? Will there be any significant changes in volume?

7 Should this scene be played in normal light? Half light? Candle light? Which will contribute best to the mood?

Try out the scene

1 Establish your performance space. The setting is Brutus's tent; consider what furniture there might be and how it would be laid out.

2 If possible, collect some props — a book, a candle, perhaps even a stringed instrument (Lucius plays the lute).

3   As you rehearse, be deliberately conscious of creating and sustaining the mood.

Extract 11: from *Woza Albert* by Percy Mtwa and Mbongeni Ngema

Woza Albert is a play written by two South African actors, Percy Mtwa and Mbongeni Ngema. They set out to show what might happen if Morena (Jesus, the preacher of peace on earth) arrived in modern South Africa for his Second Coming. The action is moving, fast moving and very funny. It consists of a lot of very short scenes showing how people of all kinds react to this momentous event. The ordinary black people are very excited, and news travels fast. The white authorities are against Morena from the start, and set out to capture him. The action follows approximately the life of Jesus. He is betrayed for a packet of chips, and sentenced to Robben Island, the notorious prison in Cape Town Harbour where many black activists have been interned.

In this scene, Morena is escaping from Robben Island, by walking on the water. Percy and Mbongeni are the crew of a military helicopter.

MBONGENI spins his hand above his head. Helicopter sounds. They are in a helicopter, looking down.

PERCY *(mimes radio)*:   Radio 1254CB receiving, over. What? That's impossible! Are you sure? Okay, over and out. Hey, what do you see down below?

MBONGENI *(miming binoculars)*:   Oh, it's a beautiful day down below. Birds are flying, swimmers are swimming, waves are waving. Hey! Morena's walking on water to Cape Town! Ag shame! His feet must be freezing! Hey, I wish I had my camera here!

PERCY: This must be the miracle of the decade!

MBONGENI: Ag, I always forget my camera!

PERCY: Down! Down! Radio 1254 CB receiving, over. Yes, we've got him. Yeah, what? Torpedo? Oh no, have a heart! He's not even disturbing the waves! Ja, I wish you could see him, he looks amazing!

MBONGENI *(nodding frantically into mike)*:   Yes man, yes!

PERCY: What? Bomb Morena? Haven't you heard what they say? You start with Morena and it's worse than an atom bomb! Over and out! Hey, this is a shit bladdy job! You pull the chain.

MBONGENI: No, you!

PERCY: No! You pull the chain!

MBONGENI: No, Man!

PERCY: This man is mos' happy, why blow him up?

MBONGENI: No, come on, come on. Fair deal! Eenie, meenie, minie moe. Vang a kaffir by the toe. As hy shrik, let him go. Eenie, meenie, minie, moe! It's you!

PERCY: Okay! This is the last straw! I think I'm resigning tomorrow!

MBONGENI: Ready ... target centre below ... release depth charges ... bombs ... torpedos ... go!

They watch. The bombs fall. A moment of silence and then a terrible explosion. They separate, come together, detonating each other.

BOTH: Mommeeee! Aunti-eeee! He-e-e-elp!

Blackout.

As you prepare to perform

Although the action of this scene could have been horrific, and the mood tragic, in fact it isn't, so don't take it too seriously — after all, Morena is bound to be resurrected!

As you set up the scene, concentrate on the moment-by-moment focusing, and don't be afraid to be inventive. The mood is meant to be manic and zany, so the wilder you can be (without losing tight focus!), the funnier the scene will be ... and the more pointed the whole satirical message.

9 Symbols

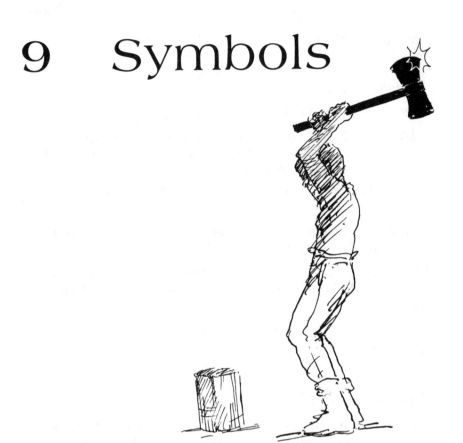

A woodcutter's axe glints in the sun as it slowly rises, then flashes down, neatly splitting a log for firewood, warmth and security. A perfect tool in the hands of a peaceful craftsman. But behind the trees lurk repression and civil war...

Symbols and meaning

To continue the story begun above, months later, driven to despair, his livelihood and his family torn from him, the same man raises his axe once more. This time, it is not to split firewood, but to strike his tormentor. The axe is now a weapon. No longer a woodcutter, he has become a revolutionary. The axe is a symbol of this change, in fact it is the central dramatic symbol of the play, summing up all that has happened.

Symbols are what the drama makes you understand —they can sum up the meaning of the play, sometimes even on a subconscious level. Symbols can be expressed through language, movement, visual images — remember the emblem you chose to symbolise the village in Chapter 7? Symbols help to reinforce the meaning of the whole experience.

Activity 1

In another last moment from an improvised drama, two people shake hands, and one says:
'Yes, but now we are equal'.
One of the hands is black.
Obviously a symbolic gesture, a summing up of what has happened. But what has happened?
In small groups suggest various scenarios which could have led to this moment being symbolic, that is, why this handshake and these words could not have taken place before this moment. Jot down the scenes as a series of titles, so you will remember them.
Now improvise that final scene leading to the climax — the moment of the handshake. Be careful not to overdo it or get melodramatic.

Gestures as symbols

Hands and how we use them already carry enormous symbolic meaning in real life. You probably know some people who seem to talk almost as much with their hands and arms as with their tongues.

Did you know a handshake probably started as a way of indicating:

'I am friendly: look and feel, I have no weapon in my right hand . . . have you?'

Activity 2

Still in the same groups, try the following gestures and see if you find a common meaning.

Cont.

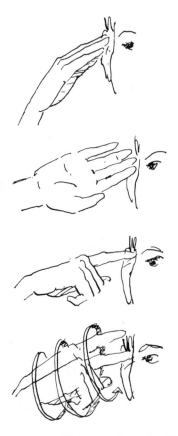

Now make a list of all the other gestures — yes, including the rude ones — which have a commonly shared symbolic meaning within the same culture.

Activity
3

Play of hands

Now go back to the scenario you developed in Activity 1. Let us capture the essence of each scene in a moment of gesture with hands. The gesture may involve many characters, or just one.

Compose these moments into a series of 'still photographs', or frozen moments. The focus of each photograph must be the hands. With as little explanation as possible, set the scene, and enact your series of stills for the rest of the class, finishing with the handshake.

Is the changing symbolism of the hands clear to an audience who does not have the benefit of knowing the story and the characters?

Objects as symbols

Some objects are very rich in symbolic association, too. A procession holding candles, for instance, is automatically more theatrical than a procession without. Add monks' hoods or masks to those holding the candles, and you already have a very powerful image. A gun is another powerful object. There is a saying in the theatre that if you have a gun on stage, you know it'll have to be used. However, no objects are dramatic symbols on their own. They must be given a meaning by the action. It's the easiest thing in the world to lump a lot of very strong symbolic images together, and maybe even fool some people that you have a powerful play or film.

Activity
4

Symbolic overload

If you have the time, have a bit of fun with symbols. In small groups or as a whole class, make a list of objects

Cont.

which automatically have strong symbolic value — a bloody dagger, a full moon, a hooting owl, a diamond ring, a snake, a rose, a lion, footprints in the snow, are a few starters. Pack as many as you can into one scene — perhaps a horror scene, or a romantic fantasy. You can include them physically, or you can mention them in the dialogue. Try to give each one its full symbolic significance. Go right over the top!

Dramatic symbols

Unlike the symbols you were just playing with, the axe and the handshake were truly dramatic symbols. The action changed them and gave them a new meaning, unique to their drama. The object, to begin with, need not be very significant at all. Shakespeare made much of a handkerchief, an unposted letter, a donkey's head, and one of the most famous films ever made (Orson Welles's *Citizen Kane*) is built round a central symbol of a child's toboggan called 'Rosebud'.

Activity 5

Create a whole-group improvisation about two communities. The tension between them will be symbolised by an object. Whatever the object, it is important to both groups, but for different reasons. The conflict is caused by misfortune, not because one group is good and the other bad.

This might give you enough to work on with your own ideas, but here is an example of a storyline you could use:

A nomadic people with their flocks need to pass through alien territory, peacefully, they hope. They see an eagle. To them, an eagle, which snatches newborn lambs, is an evil omen. So they shoot it, and offer it as part of their greeting to the resident community, little knowing that the eagle is a sacred bird of power to these people. How can the nomads make amends? What is the effect on the residents?

Try this storyline, or another of your own devising, and improvise three scenes.
- Scene 1 focuses on the symbolic object, underlining its importance.
- Scene 2 centres on the object as a tension point.
- Scene 3 resolves the conflict in such a way that the object has a new meaning for all.

Make the symbolic object real and tangible. You could make it yourselves; alternatively, you could use a symbol of the symbol! For example, a single beautiful feather will movingly evoke a dead eagle rather better than a painted plastic chicken.

And in plays . . .

Extract 12: from *The Beekeeper's Boy* by John O' Toole

The Beekeeper's Boy is a play about the childhood of Adolf Hitler. Adolf is depicted as a mother's boy, afraid and resentful of his stern father, Alois, who bullies Adolf's mother Klara. She is a gentle, obedient and loyal woman. By contrast, both Adolf and his father are obsessive. Alois's passion is bees. Adolf's obsession at this time is Red Indians, and especially 'Old Shatterhand', the violent and swaggering 'injun killer' hero of a series of novels by the German writer Karl May. In his fantasies, and in his games with his friends, Adolf has to be Shatterhand — and the leader.

This extract starts and finishes as an ordinary scene between Adolf and his mother on the family farm. The middle section is all in Adolf's imagination, as he plays out his fantasies in a game with his friends. The previous scene saw the death of Adolf's father.

ADOLF: Mama, now Papa is dead, who will look after his bees?

KLARA: I don't know, dear. Sell them or something, get rid of them.

ADOLF: Can I deal with them, Mama? I know what to do.

KLARA: Do what you like. I can't think about it now.

(*Fantasy sequence.*)

ADOLF: Once and for all. Smoke them out. Then burn the tepees.

KARL MAY: Old Shatterhand's Last Ride!

ADOLF: Ain't I the greatest. I gave them peace on the prairie. But what do I see?

KARL MAY: A plume of smoke curled up over the little homestead. Apple trees, a stream in the garden . . . and the smoking ruins of the farmhouse.

ADOLF: The Evil Ogellallahs!

KARL MAY: Old Shatterhand spat disgustedly. Then he saw the bodies. The woman still pretty in spite of ... what they'd done, sprawled in the dust with her two children ... Like their mother, they had been scalped. Old Shatterhand spat again.

ADOLF: The Ogellallahs will pay!

KARL MAY: ... he thought. There was a brooch at the woman's neck, a bunch of grapes. He stooped to read: 'Klara, with love from A.' it said. Clutching the brooch, he raised his magnificent gnarled fist to the sky.

ADOLF: I shall avenge you, Klara, whoever you are ... or were!

KARL MAY: Deep in the forest, the evil Ogellallah Indians were celebrating their dreadful triumph. On the totem pole hung three new scalps, as the braves whipped up their frenzy. Suddenly the Witchdoctor flung up his hands. The braves froze.

WITCHDOCTOR: Death! Death on the wind!

KARL MAY: He cried.

WITCHDOCTOR: Death comes like the wind and like the fire. I hear it in the whispers of the forest trees, bringing flame and destruction to our people. I hear it as our gods tremble.

CHIEF: Who challenges the gods of the Ogellallahs? Who dares challenge ME, Chief Alois Bloodhand?

KARL MAY: Silent in the snow, Shatterhand had crept close to the camp. Silently he lit his torch. The startled redskins looked around. But too late — their nemesis was upon them! Gripping his horse only with his knees as his torch swung from one hand, lighting tepee after tepee, his trusty cavalry sword in the other dripping scarlet as redskin after evil redskin met its sharp edge and bit the dust. With a final cry ...

ADOLF: Aiiiiiiiiiiiyo! I am the greatest!

KARL MAY: ... Old Shatterhand hurled the torch at the totem pole, which, with its grisly relics, blazed up; to the starlit sky.

ADOLF: (*Quietly*) At last, I am revenged.

(*Fantasy out.*)

Mama, I have dealt with Papa's hives.

KLARA: Did you sell them?

ADOLF: They're ... Nobody wanted them. I got rid of them safely. I burned them. They were no good without the bees.

KLARA: And the bees?

ADOLF: (*A touch of Shatterhand*) They won't come back.

As you prepare to perform

Think about

1 As Adolf and his friends act out their mad game, something else is really happening. What do you think Adolf is actually doing when he is 'burning the tepees'?

2 One surviving picture of Adolf's mother Klara shows her wearing a brooch with a bunch of grapes in pearl. What is the significance of that in this scene?

3 In the original production, during the 'massacre', some music was used from an opera by Wagner. It is the climax where the Hall of the Gods, Valhalla, is burned to the ground. Even as a child, Adolf Hitler was obsessed by Wagner's music. Why do you think this music was used at this point?

4 What do you think is the significance of the bees to Adolf? What do they symbolise? Considering the part Adolf Hitler was to play many years later in World War 2, and the slaughter of six million Jews, what else might be symbolised by swarms or hives of bees? (There are no 'right' answers to this question. It is left to the audience to find their own symbolic meaning.)

Try out the scene

1 You might set up your space in two quite separate parts, or use some other method, such as a lighting change, to distinguish the real from the fantasy.

2 Firstly, try the middle section purely as a fantasy. The 'bodies' are Adolf's mother, younger brother and sister, and the 'Chief' is his father. You might like to give the whole fantasy section some appropriate background music.

3 When you have played it out like this, add to it the idea that Karl May and the other people in the fantasy section are his schoolfriends, playing out a mad game of red indians with Adolf at the centre.

4 As you play the scene, look for the symbols. Remember, Adolf had a grudge against his father's harsh treatment of the family.

10 Dramatic meaning

Bones, on their own, don't mean much — there's not much life in them. Put them together, and the skeleton looks a bit like us, but simpler. Put it in a dark box, and it is scary or tragic. Prop it up on a car seat, or jiggle it to make it move, and it becomes funny.

Imagine you are a creator, and can give the skeleton life. You can flesh out the bones with whatever looks, talents and personality you like, and then you have the power to make it do whatever you want. (Dr Frankenstein discovered the perils of that, of course, when his creation got away from him!)

Meaning and truth

In drama we are the creators. Each element is like the bones of a skeleton: we can't do without them, and they only work together. The story, the situations, the people and their relationships are the flesh. Our belief in the story, and the tension which drives it, breathes life and spirit into our creation.

One of the good things about the drama we create is that it is simpler than real life. We can understand it more easily, and yet it can still be true to life.

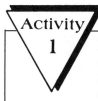

Activity 1

If you can get hold of a real skeleton, try putting it in different situations, or poses. If not, try drawing a skeleton in different situations. It will be quite easy to make it seem alive, and remind you of real life.

Reality simplified

Look back to *The Goya Drama* in chapter 5. Even today, from this distance, the events (which you probably did not know about before) are very hard to make sense of as facts. When *we* started to think about them, they came out something like this:

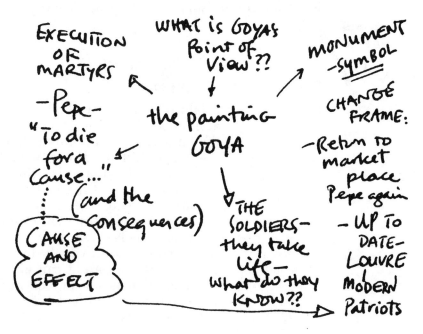

If you had actually been there in 1808, the war would have been even harder to understand. As a Spanish peasant you would not have known or cared what the French soldiers were doing there — or how they felt — you would just have hated them. As a French soldier you would probably have been bewildered and scared, just obeying orders and hearing rumours.

If *The Goya Drama* worked for you, you probably felt that you ended up with quite a clear picture, which made sense for you. You may not find it easy to put that meaning into words, but that is perfectly alright and reasonable — because whatever it means to you is a *dramatic meaning*, a mixture of the thoughts and feelings it conjured up for you.

Meaning in perspective: a Leaving School drama

There are different kinds of meaning, depending on how close to the action you are. The French soldiers will certainly feel differently from the Spanish patriots about what's happening. They will also have quite different points of view. For each, the dramatic meaning is different.

So, for the last time in this book where we are dictating the terms, we want you to experiment with the meanings that can emerge from dramatic action. The subject for our final drama, one you are probably thinking about in real life, is school: compulsory schooling and leaving school.

Scene 1

Back to school

Date: The present.

Roles: A family, not very well off, with one parent at home and the other away, or having left the family. There are three children.

- The oldest, aged seventeen, left school two years ago and is bringing home a good wage, but from a boring job.
- Twins, aged fifteen, who are still at school, but with very different ambitions: one is clever at school, and wants to go on to university to study medicine, if the parent can afford to help. The other has been looking forward to leaving, but doesn't know what to do afterwards.

All the characters are likeable, realistic people.

Establishing roles:

1   Get into groups of four and discuss, out of role, more detail about yourselves as a family.

2   Each person, go off alone and write a letter to the absent parent about your plans, your problems of the moment, and perhaps your ambitions. Let the letter help you to sympathise with the character you have taken on. It should be close to how *you* would feel in these circumstances.

3   When you have written this letter, bring it back to the family to share it with them. You will be sending the letters off together to the absent parent.

Context:

During this reading session someone turns on the television and the family hears on the news that the school leaving age has just been raised by two years, that is, no-one under 18 can leave. The law also includes those under 18 years of age who have already left school. Their jobs will be given to older unemployed people and they will have to return to school, joining the Sixth Form.

Management:

Play the scene as the family hears this news. This will demand skill in improvising, and complete concentration. You must take it slowly and seriously, or it will not develop enough impetus for you to lose yourselves in the role. The tension that develops may be your common concern and anxiety; anger and conflict may emerge.

Outcome:

1   Eventually, you will part, tear up your original letter, and write another, straight away, while still in role.

2   Out of role, piece together the bits of your first letter and compare it with the second. What has changed in your character's life?

Scene 2

School's in

During most of this book we have been exploring the serious side of drama. Now is your chance to break out! Work this scene as a whole class.

Date: The first day of the new school year.

Roles: All the twins and all the 17-year-olds stay in role. One of the parents becomes the teacher; the rest become other students, all of whom are back at school unwillingly.

Props: You will need a real dice for this scene.

Establishing roles: Students, modify your roles so that you are not so likeable. Be more of a stereotyped kid: out for yourself, smug, disobedient, dumb or feeble — decide what weakness, or unlikeable quality the person you played before might have.

If it seems unrealistic to have half a dozen sets of twins and their brothers and sisters in the same class, don't worry. This is comedy, and that touch of absurdity will add to it.

Context:	It is the first lesson back, ironically a careers lesson. All the new sixth form students, keen or reluctant, including those who were out working the year before, turn up in class together.
	The teacher arrives with some very important news:
	'Because the new leaving age has overfilled the schools, one third of every sixth form class will have to leave after all. In this lesson, you have to decide who it will be, after all, this is a democracy.'
Management:	**1** Find a way to decide who will leave, with all those who want to leave arguing their cases.
	2 The teacher needs to be allowed at least some control of the action. Don't get too rowdy, but use your role-playing skills to help each other bring out what an awful lot you are.
	3 When this has really built up to an uproar, the teacher gets a second message:
	'The Government has decreed that the most democratic way to decide who leaves is to throw a dice. The first eight people (or third of the class) who throw a six have to leave school. The teacher has to conduct this random ballot.'
	This law includes even the smug ones who want to stay!
	4 Continue the scene from the reading of the second message.
Outcome:	The lucky (or unlucky) eight get a send-off by the class while the teacher is taking the list of names to the office.
	Discuss, out of role, which moments in this scene were comic? Why and how were they funny?

The school board — 1870

In the last scene, you again looked at the advantages as well as disadvantages of staying on at school, but in a very different way from Scene 1. Now we will ask you to explore the subject

125

in a way which is true to life, but a long way from the here and now. You will be in control of the action, making your own meaning. The following information and song, 'The School Board Man', will be your data.

Background

Around 1870, compulsory schooling was introduced for the first time. Some people welcomed it, but many working-class people resented it and tried to dodge it. The song below was written by Tommy Armstrong, a parent of the time. He was a coal-miner, and was always in trouble with the hated School Board inspectors.

The School Board Man

One morning at half past eight, when the bairns [children] were
    playing at the door,
There was a man with a book in his hand, that I'd never seen
    before.
So I kindly invited him in, and to talk he soon began
And I soon got to know by the sound of his jaw
That he was the School Board Man.

He says: "Send yer Bairns to school,
      learn them all you can
      Make scholarship yer faithful friend,
      and ye'll never see the School Board Man"

He knocked on the door. I shouts "Come in."
In he comes. He says, "Good Morning Mr Armstrong."
I says, "Hold on, ye've got the wrong house."
But he wouldn't be stopped. He says, "How many children have
    you got?"
I says, "Man, that's an impudent question."
So he turns to our Bess and he says, "What family have you had?"
She says, "We've had two dead, and three alive.
        If they'd all been living, that would be five"
I says, "Are ye satisfied now? Be off or I'll flatten ye."
He never said another word till he got out of the house, then he
    puts his face against the window and he shouts:
        "Send yer bairns to school,
        learn them all ye can,
        Make scholarship yer faithful friend,
        and ye'll never see the School Board Man."

He has all the bairns in the country scared to death — and not
    only the bairns but their mother and fathers.

A few more facts

- School-age children often truanted to go to work, and the mine owners turned a blind eye — the children were cheap labour.

- Bess and Tommy Armstrong actually had thirteen children, all alive, and mostly of school age!

- To encourage schooling, any school which could prove to the School Board 90 per cent attendance for a whole week was granted a half holiday.

- Investigators of one Royal Commission looking into education for working class children "went out in groups of three to make their enquiries, only to be met by organised obstruction and hostile demonstrations (at which they saw themselves burned in effigy) by workers deeply suspicious of their motives."

- Tommy Armstrong once frightened off a female School Board inspector by coming to the door holding a huge carving knife, a dripping length of flesh-coloured sausage and with a murderous look in his eye.

- Teachers sometimes tried to cover up for the children who were truanting, so the School Board inspectors would come to the schools and check the children's slates.

- Not all working class parents found the teachers acceptable. One early Inspector of Schools found "a very deaf hunchback as master of a school in Yorkshire. The explanation was that if such a man were employed as a teacher, at least the parish had no need to put him on the Poor Rate."[2]

- Parents of truants were fined 7 shillings and 6 pence, a lot for a working family in those days, and had to travel to the Assize Court, losing a day's pay. They could be sent to prison for repeated offences.

- The behaviour of people like the Armstrongs was the despair of many middle-class people, who hoped that compulsory schooling would help the working class 'to better themselves'.

[1] Simon B. (1960) *History of Education 1780–1870*, London, Lawrence and Wishart (p. 72).
[2] Musgrave, P.W. (1968) *Society and Education in England since 1800*, London, Methuen.

Scene 3

School's in — 1870
A historical documentary

1 Get into groups of about six to eight. Each group is a television documentary team of producers, actors and presenters.

2 Use the song and data above to make a short documentary feature programme, live or on video, on this piece of history. To make it easier, you may invent whatever you like that will flesh out your context.

3 In your production team, first agree on your attitude to this data.

- Are you on the side of the parents and children who thought they should not have to go to school?
- Do you think, like the School Board, that compulsory schooling was or is a good thing?
- Do you want to stay neutral and present both sides of the case?

4 Now look again at the data, and see what you could use as your starting point. You do not have to stick to the Armstrongs. Feel free to invent any scene you like which is in keeping with the data. You could devise interviews with Tommy or Bess Armstrong, or some children of the time, a School Board inspector, a Member of Parliament, or a teacher.

You could set a scene at a mine or a factory, or in a school where the children who did not want to be there could make things very difficult for the teacher!

5 You could set your piece entirely in 1870, or you could use a 'then and now' approach, comparing scenes of truanting and punishment with the present day.

6 You may want to make your documentary as realistic as possible, or you may wish to use comedy (as Tommy Armstrong does). You can also use both approaches in contrast, to make your dramatic reconstruction entertaining and interesting.

Playing with meaning

As we said before you started these scenes, there are different kinds of dramatic meaning depending on how close you feel to the action. Each of the three scenes gave you a view into the same subject: compulsory schooling.

In the first, 'Back to school', you probably felt sympathy for the characters. If it really worked, you would be living the roles with them, while you were playing the scene. In the second, 'School's in', you are probably glad that you were not really in that situation, as one of those dreadful characters. In the third, 'School's in: 1870', you had the choice throughout, about how you felt and what you wanted the action to say.

If you look at the diagram, 'Framing the participants', you will see that it looks very similar to our framing diagram on page 39. That diagram showed how dramatic action can be set within, on the edge of, or right outside the event or story. This diagram shows how the participants of a role-play (or spectators of a play) can also be placed inside or outside the story.

Inside the action

We can be made to forget our real selves, to live the action with the characters as we identify with them. This is how adventure stories, tragedies, soap operas and most improvisations in this book work. It is real for us at the moment of happening, and we often call it realism.

Framing the participant

Outside the action

We can see what is happening, and even feel the tension, but we are detached enough to laugh at it or reflect on it. This is how comedy works, showing people's weaknesses. We are glad we are not hanging off a twenty-storey building with our trousers coming down. It is also how satire works, where we can see what is wrong, although the characters can't.

Controlling the action

Further off still, we can be detached enough to manipulate the story. Still in the dramatic context, we can change it, experiment with it or highlight particular aspects. This is how parody and send-up works. It is also how documentary drama works.

Activity 2

After a very hard few paragraphs — hard because we have reached the centre of what drama is all about — a very easy activity.

Make a copy of the diagram on page 130, leaving out the illustrations. Now fill in the three scenes in whichever frame you think each should fit. When you have done that, think of some of the dramas you know or have done — plays, films, improvisation, television programmes. Now fit them into the appropriate frame. Some frames will get fuller than others, depending on what your taste is in drama!

And in plays . . .

Extract 13: from *The Fourth Year Are Animals*

To find a short piece of play text that illustrates dramatic meaning is of course very difficult. As we have seen throughout this book, meaning is made up of all the other elements, and emerges gradually. However, if we are to look for it anywhere, it is likely to be at the end.

The playwright resolves the story and the tensions in a way that is right for him or her. Sometimes the playwright's ending is only one of several possible. You may have noticed that the ending of a play or film is what the audience most often argues about:

'I wish it had ended happily' . . .

'No that would have been slack, it was more real . . . etc'.

We are reprinting the ending of *The Fourth Year Are Animals* in case you have not been able to study the whole play. Of course, it will be much better if you have read it right through, so you can see how the ending is a result of everything that has happened before.

Things have gone from bad to worse for Alan with his fourth year class, in spite of his idealistic hopes. He and Kelly are at war. Driven into ruthlessly asserting his authority in a dictation exercise, he makes his greatest mistake: Arthur, in spite of instructions to the contrary, keeps putting his hand up.

ALAN: Arthur, if you don't know something leave a space. 'Cold comma sodden boots in wet grass . . . cold comma sodden boots in wet grass . . . comma . . .' I said leave a space Arthur. And put your hand down before I throw something at you!

(ARTHUR *puts his hand down.*)

'. . . Rain trickling down our necks . . . rain trickling down our necks . . .'

(ARTHUR'S *hand is up again.* ALAN *ignores it.*)

'. . . we pressed forward in the darkness . . . we pressed forward in the darkness . . .'

(ARTHUR *slumps forward, holding his head in his hands.* KELLY *notices him and whispers to* THERESA *as* ALAN *continues . . .*)

'. . ignorant of the unseen horror . . . ignorant of the unseen horror . . . that sooner or later . . . that sooner or later . . .'

(THERESA *and* KELLY *have both stopped writing.* ALAN *slams the desk lid.*)

What the hell do you think you're playing at?

KELLY: It's Arthur, Sir.

ALAN: What is it Arthur?

KELLY: He's pissed in his pants, Sir.

(ALAN *realises the awful truth.*)

ALAN: Get out the rest of you.

KELLY: Where will we go, Sir?

ALAN: I don't care — just get out.

(THERESA *and* KELLY *exit.* ARTHUR *remains, head down.* ALAN *is now quite unable to cope with the situation.*)

ARTHUR: I didn't mean to piss, Sir.

ALAN: I know that . . . would you like to go home? I'll explain to . . . who have you got after lunch?

ARTHUR: The other kids would only say that I . . .

ALAN: Don't worry what the other kids say.

(*Pause. KELLY returns and stands outside the door. She carries a tracksuit bottom.*)

I really am sorry Arthur.

(*He notices KELLY.*)

What are you staring at?

KELLY: I just brought a tracksuit bottom for Arthur.

ALAN: Oh.

(*He moves to take it from her, but she pushes past him and gives it to ARTHUR herself. ARTHUR pulls it on over his trousers.*)

Now come on, I'll give you a lift home. .

ARTHUR: It's alright Sir, I'll walk.

(*ARTHUR limps off. ALAN looks after him, still wondering whether to follow or to leave ARTHUR alone.*)

KELLY: He'll be alright Sir, I reckon. You should have let him go before he did it . . . Arthur's got this problem . . .

ALAN: (*Angrily and guiltily*) I know, Kelly. So I made a mistake, Okay? Everyone else makes mistakes — why shouldn't I? I'm only human.

(*He sinks down in a chair, turning his face away from her.*)

(*Quietly*) I'm only human.

(*Long pause, then . . .*)

KELLY: Sir — You're a good bloke Sir.

(*ALAN turns and stares to see if she is kidding. She isn't.*)

When are we going to do Drama again, Sir?

ALAN: We'll see.

(*She smiles. ALAN smiles back and they exit together.*)

Preparing to perform — your way

And that is how Richard Tulloch ended his encounter with the 4th form animals. It was a play originally written and performed for a high school audience, and an important part of his message is that both teachers and students are 'only human'.

Think about

1 The dictation piece is symbolic of the action in this scene. Can you see the double meaning in it?

2 Earlier on, the playwright has already shown that Kelly has a kinder side. Where?

3 This final scene leaves us wondering what happens next.
- Is this a happy ending where Kelly and Alan will be nice to each other from now on?
- How do you think their relationship will develop from this point?

4 You may have come across school situations where the war between the Kellys and the Alans was worse than this. After the total humiliation of Alan, it is quite a surprise when Kelly softens towards him.
- If you were a cynical student or teacher at such a school, do you think this ending would satisfy you?
- If it wouldn't, how would you end the play?

Try out the scene

Within your group, people will probably have different opinions about this ending. In productions, the audience often has a lively debate on how realistic it is. If there are divided opinions about the ending, break into small groups and take one of the following approaches.

1 If, for you, this ending is right, get ready to act it out. Your first priority is to ensure that the sudden softening between Kelly and Alan is believable. Establish that they act this way because they are basically nice people who tend to act on impulse and have more in common than they admit.

2 If, on the other hand, you think that in real life this ending would be unlikely to happen, devise an alternative ending for yourselves. This must be one which fits the characters of Kelly, Alan and Arthur, as you see them. It must also round off the play. You will need to use group discussion and improvisation for this approach. When you are satisfied with your ending, prepare to act it out.

Now act out both versions of the ending. Have the people who used Richard Tulloch's ending made it believable? Have the people who created their own endings made their versions believable? Have they changed the message of the whole play?

11 Improvisation as art

Now you understand the bones of drama. You have already been making the skeleton dance, and you are quite ready to start making your own dramatic creations, flesh and blood and all. This chapter outlines how the elements of drama can be used to improvise dramas for your own exploration and discovery.

Making a start

In this book we have frequently used role-plays and improvisation to explore the elements of drama, shaping action by controlling and manipulating those elements. As the improvisations grew we explored themes: the topic of winning and losing in *An Olympics Drama*, national pride in *The Goya Drama* and education in *The Leaving School Drama*.

You and your classmates can now select the topics you want to explore and investigate. Improvisation requires you to select a topic and then explore it in action. In this way improvising around a topic is very different from just discussing it or writing around it. Your exploration uses dramatic action to create its own dramatic meaning.

So, now it is time to use your understanding of drama to explore topics of your own choosing from the world in which you live.

Sources for improvisations

Where to find ideas and topics to explore? At first it may seem there is little you want to base a drama around. Don't worry, there are millions of dramas out there just waiting to happen, and with the right skills and commitment you can make them happen. This list will give you many starting points.

An A to Z of improvisation

A Advertisements

B Books and novels

C Cartoons

D Documents

E Entries in diaries or journals

F Funeral notices

G Government statements

H Holograms and photographs

I Images (frozen tableaux)

J Just the headline

K Koran and other books of knowledge

L Letters — personal or 'to the editor'

M Myths

N Newspaper articles

O Oral accounts and histories

P Pop songs

Q Quality films — or even poor ones

R Rules and regulations

S Sculptures and paintings

T Television programmes

U Useful objects and items

V Verse and poetry

W Wise sayings — proverbs

X X-tremely good or bad plays

Y Yellow Pages

Z Zodiac signs and the stars

Isolating a theme

That A to Z of improvisation will give you plenty of sources for your dramas. Often a group will find that there are quite a number of topics put forward by participants, more than can be handled in one drama. One drama class recently listed the following topics:
- child abuse
- cruelty to living things
- soap operas
- nuclear war
- the irony of criticism
- double standards.

Clearly not all of these topics could be considered in one drama, so the class isolated one using the following steps.

1 They discussed all topics and suggested possible ways of focusing the action. All topics were listed on the blackboard.

2 Attempts were made to group topics which seemed to go together.

3   The class voted on which topic it would select. They voted a couple of times, each time eliminating those with the smallest number of votes. Finally one topic had a majority of class support — nuclear war.

You may wish to follow similar steps to isolate a topic for your group.

Journal keeping

During some of our earlier dramas we have referred to the importance of documentation. As you use your drama skills to create action around your particular topic, it is helpful to keep a journal of the complete work, recording the action and your analysis of it. Such a journal is best completed after each session and contains:
- a brief description of the action
- any discoveries you made and feelings you experienced
- your evaluation of the way the elements of drama were managed — especially when there are problems with the drama.

Your journal will help you analyse the action and see how the elements of drama are working. It will also help you reflect on what the drama means for you: on the dramatic meaning you are creating. Later we will see some extracts from the journals of students who took part in the nuclear war drama.

Managing the improvisation

Before you start you should have an idea of the time available to you for the improvisation. You may spend a week on a particular topic, or at times you may have longer. The nuclear war drama lasted for sixteen lessons over about a month.

Any improvisation which is built by 20 to 30 people over a long period of time poses a huge dramatic challenge for the participants. Clearly the building process needs to be managed carefully, otherwise the work may become disorganised and lack direction.

For a group to work successfully in this way trust between group members is crucial, as is a shared commitment to the topic and the drama. The points raised on page 2 in 'How the drama group works' also apply in an extended improvised project.

An improvisation can be managed in two ways.
- *Inside the action* — changes are introduced during the drama, while the participants are in role.

- *Outside the action* — changes are decided upon after the action has been temporarily stopped, while participants are out of role.

Inside the action

After an improvisation has been set up — roles established, tensions introduced, focus selected and time and place clarified — participants may introduce new material or ideas spontaneously, during the action. Of course such input must be constructive; it must stem from the drama and advance the action.

Commitment and co-operation

When managing an improvisation from within the action each participant is responsible for the drama, and all participants must take care of it. It only takes one member of the group to destroy a drama — by inventing an easy solution to a problem, or participating in an inappropriate way, eg suddenly pretending to be drunk. It's up to you all — take care of the drama!

Not all participants can be leaders. Working constructively does not mean taking control and forcing everyone to be in *your* drama. The action belongs to the group, which means that each participant will sometimes take the initiative, at other times follow someone else's lead.

After one successful session of the nuclear war drama a participant wrote, 'Everyone seemed to realise that to contribute to the drama did not require taking charge or making loud statements. Most people assumed minor, although still highly productive roles.' (Christy)

Maintaining focus

Focus is the element of drama which can most easily be lost as action develops. Be alert for ways of focusing the action, and when a focus emerges follow it. Here is another comment regarding the nuclear war drama: '... any attempts to focus the drama (for example when the meeting was called, and later when the food expedition was organised) failed because not everybody was involved, and not everybody supported it.' (Kym)

Outside the action

The most common means of managing an improvisation is by stopping the action and talking about it, discussing what happened, how good it was and where it should develop next. Such talks can be held with the whole group, in small groups or in pairs. Talking about the drama can often help you understand what occurred in it. And, as we mentioned earlier, keeping a journal also helps us to reflect, individually, upon all these aspects.

How the elements of drama are used

When we focus on how the elements of drama are being used we can see where the strong points and the weak spots are. The following extracts are from the journals of students who participated in the nuclear war drama.

'There were some short *focuses*, eg when Colin was talking about the radiation cure, when they told us the air filter wasn't working anymore; but it didn't last long. We need a long term focus.' (Karelia)

'There was a little loss of *tension* here as the three didn't really know what to do. They tried giving us jobs and so on. It would have been good if one of them joined forces with us.' (Melek)

'The last of these guards created a *symbol* of power with the microphone. They wouldn't let him have it.' (Kym)

'On Friday we're going to cover the windows, decrease the *space* and create machinery, eg air filters. We are going to bring useful items into the next lesson, eg blankets.' (Carlie)

'After a while Aaron stopped the drama and it was decided that there was no *focus*, and it was just drifting on.' (Katherine)

'We agreed the *tension* was strongest right at the end when we were standing around wondering what to do with the dead bodies.' (Karelia)

Future directions

Again, through discussion, we can work out new directions our drama needs to take, new material to be researched. For example our topic may demand that we find out more factual information to substantiate the drama: in the nuclear war drama, students decided they needed to watch television programmes on nuclear war, fallout shelters and the effects of atomic explosions. Again extracts from the student journals will illustrate this process.

'Christy had the very good suggestion of somehow handicapping ourselves, and we decided on making a blindfold with holes cut to give limited vision. We'll be trying this idea next lesson.' (Fiona)

'This was a lesson in which we discussed what was to be our next drama. It was a lesson in which we were in complete control. There were lots of good ideas suggested and we eventually decided that we would start a drama which is based after a nuclear holocaust, and most of the survivors handicapped in some way. In the drama I'm partially blinded due to radiation and I'm also suffering hair loss.' (Michelle)

'We saw another film on nuclear war/aftermath. I think these films are really useful in our improvisation because they give us a factual backing to our drama.' (Briggita)

De-roling

When you are involved in a powerful drama you will be experiencing strong, real emotions. At the end, you may feel the need to stop, take a breath, and discuss what happened. This is called de-roling. Often, a de-roling session is full of excitement and laughter as you recall, and maybe even send up, the key tensions and moments.

Sometimes you may prefer to be alone to reflect on the drama and what it means to you. You may feel like channeling the energy into another activity — writing a poem or a song, making a painting — or something energetic like a game of basketball or running a marathon! Again, writing in a journal is an excellent way of clarifying things, and we close this chapter with some more journal extracts from the nuclear war drama.

'The drama drained me emotionally. However I hope we don't try to reconstruct it. I think we should leave it as it is and think about another aspect. To reconstruct would be like destroying it.' (Kim)

'I think the improvisation was a valuable one and the strongest and bleakest I'd been involved in.' (Katherine)

'All through the improvisation I was scared witless. The sudden realisation that this might happen, that this supposedly over-exaggerated drama could actually come alive one day. What we did was actually under-exaggerated. It's all very frightening.' (Kathy)

'I loved every minute of the drama today! I thought it was the best one we've ever done. It really got your emotions involved thinking "What would happen to disabled people in a civilisation where survival of the fittest was the most practical way of living".' (Fiona)

12 Improvisation towards performance

As we said at the beginning of this book, the most exciting discoveries in drama are made once you agree to step into that imaginary world of your own making. But perhaps you would like now to turn your improvised drama into a public performance: flesh out the bones of the monster you have created. This final chapter will show you how. Go to it Dr Frankenstein!

Drama — public and private

You will have noticed that throughout this book we have usually kept the improvisation work quite separate from the texts of plays. The elements of drama are the same, but there are important differences.

In an improvisation you are involved in the event; it is happening now for your satisfaction. Outsiders often have no idea of its power, or even what is happening.

- It is changing and developing as it happens.
- You are exploring and discovering as it happens.

On the other hand, in a play you are performing something for other people, an audience.

- You must know in advance what thing you are showing — it needs to be scripted and rehearsed.
- For the audience to understand and enjoy it, the meaning must be visible. They must see the people, the place, the movement and the symbols; follow the narrative; hear the language; feel the tension and the mood.

These two faces of drama can be represented by the following diagram.

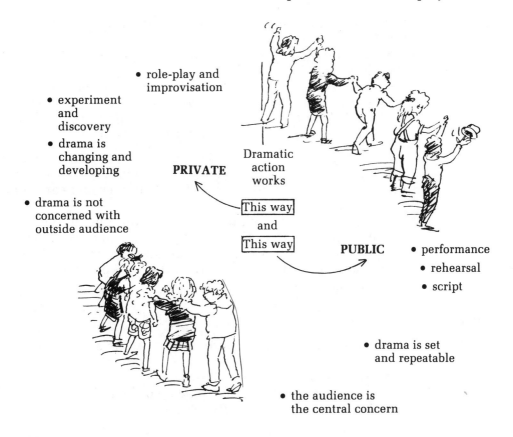

- experiment and discovery
- drama is changing and developing

- role-play and improvisation

PRIVATE

- drama is not concerned with outside audience

Dramatic action works

This way

and

This way

PUBLIC

- performance
- rehearsal
- script

- drama is set and repeatable

- the audience is the central concern

Building a play

In improvisation, spontaneity is very important; in a play the rehearsal process makes it a less important feature. Improvisation is a good way to start building a play, however. Nowadays many playwrights work with a team of actors, improvising the script as they go. But there is usually more to creating a finished play than just 'polishing up' an improvisation. Doing that, you are in danger of losing the tension as you lose the spontaneity. We recommend a series of steps.

Step 1: Improvisation and research

Go back to the A to Z list on pages 135–6 and decide on a topic. Set up whatever improvisations you think will help you to explore and understand the topic — why people react like that, why it should happen, etc. Don't forget to make use of the techniques we introduced in earlier chapters. This book is your resource. Use it.

At the same time, do all the research you can to find out more about your topic.

- Read up all you can find on the subject, view films and videos.
- Talk to other people who might have information. And if you find people who do, tape record them. Their words can be very valuable, and because they are speaking, their language is direct and often dramatic.

Some topics you can go and experience for yourselves. For a play set in a circus, for instance, you should go and soak up the atmosphere of a circus, keeping your eyes and ears wide open for interesting details.

In this whole research process you should be on the look-out for striking details. Don't worry if you don't see how they fit in yet, just make a note of them. Trust your instinct — if they seem interesting or arresting, they are probably important and usable somewhere.

Step 2: Finding a line

Start bringing into your improvisations some of the research. For example:

- focus on one striking detail
- set up a scene based on a tape recording
- reconstruct your real life experience.

As you do this, start looking for a clear line through, by way of a story, or a special message. The following should emerge, and need to be decided upon now.

What and **why** — what you want to say about the topic and why an audience should want to know about it.

Who — the important characters.

Where — the location of the action, your setting.

When — the timeline of your story, the cause and effect.

An overall shape may emerge here, depending on your topic. There is another question to be decided at this point, as well:

Who to — who will be your audience? Friends and people your own age? Parents and familiar adults? Adult strangers? Young children? Old people? Street crowds? A specialised audience like a football club or hospital patients? Each of these will want a different kind of play, though your basic message may be the same.

Step 3: From drama to theatre — finding a style

When you have established the what and why, who, where, when — and who to, you can start experimenting to find a

style. Single out those improvisations which were most significant. You will need to modify them, so that they:
- have maximum power and tension
- become clear to outsiders.

How you decide on a style depends on whether you want the drama to be realistic or stylised. You may experiment with both, or you may know already which one suits your topic.

Realism

1 Re-enact the improvisation — more than once if necessary. Appoint a couple of monitors to watch and note down:
- the most important moments
- particularly effective words or dialogue
- crucial movements
- any symbols which emerge
- the gains and losses.

Share your impressions afterwards, and begin to shape the scenes.

2 Now re-enact each scene again, with these constraints:
- all those points that were considered important must remain
- all words must be heard by your outside monitors
- all unnecessary or confusing words, talk and movements must be cut out.

It is a very good idea to tape, preferably videotape, this stage.

3 Now review and decide if the focus is clear. Is the piece long enough to develop tension, but not so long that it loses it? What may need to be added, to make it clearer, or more powerful? What could be cut even further without losing anything? Be brutal with yourselves here!

Realism on stage

Following these steps, you can gradually build up a realistic play. As well, your instinct should tell you whether you need to rearrange scenes, add new ones, or drop ones which do not seem to be working. Bear in mind your chosen audience, what they will need to keep them interested.

Realism is not easy, however. You may find that by making these modifications your scenes now seem artificial. This is because a stage is not a very realistic place. We are so used to seeing films and television shows with entirely realistic settings or real locations, using actors who are trained and experienced, that realism on stage can be a letdown. The strength of the feeling in your original improvisation may now appear limp and lacking in impact as you lose the spontaneity.

There is another way: to move away from realism and use the power of drama to create startling images and contrasts.

Stylisation

Take a scene from your original improvisation, and try a few of the following exercises — some of them will not be at all appropriate for your particular topic; you will know which.

Movement with narrator

The narrator tells the story of the scene using the third person (he, she and they), while the characters mime the actions. The narrator may speak coolly and objectively.

Cutting the language down

Each character writes down the two sentences from the original scene which most strongly show his or her position or feeling. Now, these become the only words that can be used. The order of the words can be changed, they can be split up and shuffled, and repeated as often as you like — the whole sentences or just one word.

Now try to re-enact the scene to make the meaning clear. You will find that you have to reorganise the movements completely, and it will not be at all realistic.

Movement alone

Enact the scene with no words at all, seeing if you can make it clear to a monitor who does not know the content. Experiment with this. You will find that just realistic movement, like shaking your fists and tearing your hair in an argument, for instance, will probably not get you very far. Make your movements more symbolic: use a drum or appropriate music to help. Use a prop to denote a focus of discussion, perhaps. Use different levels to show changing status.

A specialised style

Turn the scene, or the whole story, into a fairy story, a Victorian melodrama, a musical song and dance show, a puppet show (using yourselves as puppets!). There are many other different forms you could use.

Changing the location or time

Re-enact your story in an entirely different place or time, but one where it might have happened: the Stone Age, King Arthur's court, the planet Betelgeuse or London in 3001 AD.

Changing the frame

Enact the story as if it is being told to a psychiatrist, with flashbacks. Or treat it as a legend, being retold by descendants, who now have very different values, poking fun at their extraordinary ancestors. Again as a legend, make it part of a very important ceremony (remember this is what we did in Chapter 7).

Step 4: Making the play

Whichever method you chose, realism or stylisation, your play should by now have taken shape. As a check, go back to the skeleton diagram, 'The elements of drama', facing page 1, and see that the elements are all in place.

The outline of a script will probably have emerged. If you are working in realism you may prefer not to create too tight a script. You may be able to keep it fresher without one, providing that the characters, their motivations and the dramatic action are clear enough. If you have stylised it, you will need to have a very exact script, because timing, contrast and images need to be crystal clear.

However you are writing your script, make sure that it holds together. This is particularly important if several people are involved. You need to keep in close contact with each other throughout, and be very critical of the work (as critical as you can without falling out!).

You may be able to start production before your script is finished. However big or small your play (and for a first effort, half an hour or less is probably quite enough), you must do it justice by producing it properly and with absolute care. This is only fair to yourselves, after all the work you have put in. It is also only fair to your audience. You are expecting to take half an hour out of their lives to watch your drama, and probably making them pay for the privilege.

If you have fleshed out and clothed the skeleton properly, it *will* be a privilege. After all, drama tells us about ourselves, about humans. Whether we are sharing it among ourselves, in improvisation, or with others, in performance, drama is there to be shared.

Acknowledgements

The authors and publishers would like to thank the following for permission to reproduce copyright material in this book:

Aboriginal Arts Board for the painting by Mary Joseph;

Heinemann Educational Books Ltd for the extract from *The Children's Crusade* by Paul Thompson;

Museo Del Prado, Madrid, for Goya's *The Third of May*;

Oxford University Press for the extract from *The Insect Play* by Josef and Karel Capek, translated by Paul Selver, 1961;

Playlab Press Brisbane for the extract from *The Beekeeper's Boy* by John O'Toole;

Tessa Sayle for the extract from *Oh What a Lovely War*, © 1965 by Joan Littlewood's Theatre Workshop with Charles Chilton after a stage treatment by Ted Allan;

The Sunday Mail, Brisbane, for 'The day the tears flowed' (12 August 1984);

Heinemann Publishers Australia Pty Ltd and Cambridge University Press for *The Fourth Year are Animals* by Richard Tulloch;

Methuen and Co Ltd for *Woza Albert*.